HIDE AND SEEK
THE PSYCHOLOGY OF
SELF-DECEPTION

What we believe to be the motives of our conduct are usually but the pretexts for it.

Miguel de Unamuno

Every life is, more or less, a ruin among whose debris we have to discover what the person ought to have been.

José Ortega y Gasset

HIDE AND SEEK

THE PSYCHOLOGY
OF SELF-DECEPTION

Neel Burton

Acheron Press

Flectere si nequeo superos
Acheronta movebo

First published by Acheron Press in 2012
Reprinted in 2015 and 2016

A CIP catalogue record for this book is available from the British Library.

ISBN 978 0 9560353 6 3

Typeset by Phoenix Photosetting, Chatham, Kent, United Kingdom
Printed and bound by SRP Limited, Exeter, Devon, United Kingdom

About Neel Burton

Neel Burton is a psychiatrist, philosopher, writer, and wine-lover who lives and teaches in Oxford, England. He is a Fellow of Green-Templeton College, Oxford, and the recipient of the Society of Authors' Richard Asher Prize, the British Medical Association's Young Authors' Award, the Medical Journalists' Association Open Book Award, and a Best in the World Gourmand Award. His other books include *The Art of Failure*, *The Meaning of Madness, Plato's Shadow*, and *Heaven and Hell: The Psychology of the Emotions*.

www.neelburton.com

About Acheron Press

Acheron Press was established in 2008 by Neel Burton for the purpose of producing and publishing challenging, thought-provoking books without the several constraints of a commercial, sales-driven approach.

The name 'Acheron' was inspired by a verse from the Aeneid:

Flectere si nequeo superos, Acheronta movebo

The line is often translated as, 'if I cannot bend Heaven, I shall move Hell', and was chosen by Freud as the epigraph to his *Interpretation of Dreams*.

According to the psychoanalyst Bruno Bettelheim, the line encapsulates Freud's theory that people who have no control over the outside world turn inward to the underworld of their own minds.

Contents

Contents

Introduction

Self-deception is something that I have spent a long time thinking about, that I see a lot in others, and that I am still, inevitably, prone to. It is important not only because it is common and universal, but also because it is responsible for the vast majority of human tragedies, both tragedies of commission and of omission. Of course, the science of self-deception can help us to live better and get more out of life. But it can also cast a murky light on human nature and the human condition, for example, on such exclusively human phenomena as anger, depression, fear, pity, pride, dream making, love making, and god making, not to forget age-old philosophical problems such as selfhood, virtue, happiness, and the good life. I don't think anything could possibly be more important.

At the same time, I should also issue something of a health warning. Some people might find *Hide and Seek* difficult to read, perhaps even more so than they did my previous books *The Art of Failure* and *The Meaning of Madness* (if they have read them). Although these three books are not particularly intellectually demanding, they can at times be very emotionally challenging – especially to those who have seldom had the time, strength, humility, or misfortune to examine their deepest thoughts and feelings. All three books can provoke violent reactions, but this one all the more so for being about the violent reactions themselves. It is not one for the faint-hearted, lily-livered, or yellow-bellied.

Hide and Seek has been organized into 38 chapters and four parts. The 38 chapters of the book are mostly although not exclusively constructed around the unconscious ego defences recognized by Sigmund Freud and others. I have chosen to discuss self-deception in terms of ego defences because most thinking on the subject of self-deception has been undertaken in these terms. This, happily, is just as it should be. In the final analysis, all means of self-deception can be understood as methods of protecting or enhancing the ego. For example, a person who buys a £10,000 watch instead of a £1000 watch because 'you can really tell the difference in quality' is (most probably) both disguising his embarrassing craving to be loved and at the same time holding it up in the form of a virtue. The four parts of the book correspond to the four major groups of ego defences that I have identified, and represent four basic operations – namely, abstraction, transformation, evasion, and projection – for minimizing threats to the ego and, in particular, for minimizing the fear and anxiety that these threats give rise to. I have not discussed every ego defence that has ever been identified, but only the most important or interesting ones. In any case, many if not most of the ego defences that I have left out can be interpreted as subtypes of other, more basic or important ego defences that I have of course made sure to cover.

Finally, just a short note of excuse to say that I have used the male pronoun throughout, not, of course, out of an innate belief in the superiority of man over woman, but out of a desire for clarity and a reverence for the English language.

PART I: ABSTRACTION

Abstraction involves trying to ignore or suppress the source of the anxiety so that it, and therefore the anxiety, no longer seems to exist. All of the ego defences discussed in this first section aim, or aim primarily, at abstraction.

1. Denial

Denial, a term that is often dropped into casual conversation, is the simple refusal to admit to certain unacceptable or unmanageable aspects of reality, even in the face of overwhelming evidence for their existence. An example of denial is a middle-aged physician who ignores the classic signs and symptoms of a heart attack[1] and casually continues with his game of golf.

Here is a second, much more vivid – not to say sordid – example of denial. In September 2007, the British press reported on an unusually macabre story. Ten years earlier, a widow had died at the age of 84 from an embolism brought on by a thrombosis in one of the veins in her legs. However, the widow's two middle-aged daughters queried this cause of death, and asked the funeral parlour to keep their mother's cadaver in cold storage. The initial purpose for this request

---

1   Crushing central chest pain radiating into the left arm and associated with sweating, shortness of breath, and nausea.

had been to obtain a second opinion, but ten years later the cadaver had still not been interred. Instead, the daughters had been having the cadaver brought out into a chapel of rest to be visited by them at regular intervals. The younger sister, a bank worker, visited every Saturday lunch-time to sit with the cadaver; the elder sister, a caterer, visited separately to touch up her mum's lipstick and foundation and to place fresh padding in her stomach cavity. With the passing years, the cadaver had decomposed into little more than a skeleton with a bit of stretched, scaly skin over the head and upper body. This unconventional although entirely legal arrangement had so far cost the sisters an estimated £13,600 in fees, replacement coffins, and make-up. A source from within the family told the press, 'They don't seem to think that what they're doing is in any way bizarre, but it's disturbing.' The local vicar added, 'I did not know this was happening but I worry what this is doing to the two daughters. They are in denial and it cannot be helping them in their grieving process. 'Perhaps they are numb to it now after ten years but I hope it ends for their sake. 'I have never heard of anything like this before. It is not like visiting a grave at all, it is a denial that death has happened – most troubling.'

In her book of 1969, *On Death and Dying*, the psychiatrist Elisabeth Kübler-Ross introduced a model commonly referred to as The Five Stages of Grief. This model describes, in five discrete stages – namely, denial, anger, bargaining, depression (or grieving), and acceptance – a process by which people react to grief and tragedy, and in particular to terminal illness or catastrophic loss. Just as it is possible for a person to move back and forth between the stages, often several times and at great speed, so it is possible for him to get stuck in one of the earlier stages, failing to come to terms with his loss or fate. The model has been criticized on a number of grounds, but Kübler-Ross did emphasise that not all five stages need occur in the order given, or indeed occur at all, and that reactions to illness, death, and loss are as diverse as the people experiencing them.

Denial is also especially common in people with alcohol or drug dependence, and, as in all cases of denial, direct confrontation is only likely to lead to anger and resentment. Instead of direct confrontation a more gentle and tangential approach should be preferred so as to encourage the person both to challenge his beliefs and to motivate himself for change. Ideally, a typical five-minute general practice consultation might go something like this,

> Doctor: *We all enjoy a drink now and then, but sometimes alcohol can do us a lot of harm. What do you know about the harmful effects of alcohol?*
> Patient: *Quite a bit, I'm afraid. My best friend, well, he used to drink a lot. Last year he spent three months in hospital. I visited him often, but*

9

most of the time he wasn't with it. Then he died from internal bleeding.

D: *I'm sorry to hear that, alcohol can really do us a lot of damage.*

P: *It does a lot of damage to the liver, doesn't it?*

D: *That's right, but it doesn't just damage our body. It also damages our lives: our work, our finances, our relationships.*

P: *Funny you should say that. My wife's been at my neck ...*

(...)

D: *So you've told me that you're currently drinking about 16 units of alcohol a day. This has placed severe strain on your marriage and on your relationship with your daughter Emma, not to mention that you haven't been to work since last Tuesday and have started to fear for your job. But what you fear most is ending up lying on a hospital bed like your friend Tom. Is that a fair summary of things as they stand?*

P: *Things are completely out of hand, aren't they? If I don't stop drinking now, I might lose everything I've built over the past 20 years: my job, my marriage, even my daughter.*

D: *I'm afraid you might be right.*

P: *I really need to quit drinking.*

D: *You sound very determined. Why don't we make*

> *another appointment to talk about the ways in which we might support you?*

In this scenario, the doctor is using a counselling approach called 'motivational interviewing' (MI), which is generally used by psychiatrists and other healthcare professionals to get a person round to reducing his alcohol or drug intake. However, the technique has very broad applications. In our private life, we often feel compelled to offer advice to our near and dear, but the better the advice, the more likely it is to hit a nerve and to be ignored, resisted, or opposed. This can have unfortunate consequences, not only for the problem in hand but also for the warmth and, in some cases, the sustainability of the relationship.

Such pitfalls can be avoided by using the principles and techniques of MI. In short, MI involves a sort of open, non-judgemental, and empathetic style of questioning aimed first at determining a person's readiness for change and then, if possible, at (1) encouraging him to recognize the full import of his problem and (2) guiding his reasoning so that he appears to come to a solution all by himself. This not only helps him to recognize and address the problem, but also strengthens rather than undermines the relationship or, in the professional setting, the 'therapeutic alliance'. In contrast, the alternative of direct confrontation hardly bears thinking about:

Doctor: *According to your blood tests, it seems your drinking too much alcohol.*

Patient: *I suppose I do enjoy the odd drink.*

D: *You're probably having far more than just the odd drink. Alcohol is very bad for you, you need to stop drinking.*

P: *You sound like my wife.*

D: *Well, she's right you know. Alcohol can cause liver and heart problems and many other things besides. So you really need to stop drinking, OK?*

P: *Yes, doctor, thank you.* (Patient never returns.)

Sigmund Freud first formulated the concept of denial. His daughter Anna Freud thought of it as an immature ego defence, first, in that it is especially used in childhood and adolescence and, second, in that its continued use into adulthood leads to inappropriate and maladaptive behaviours and to a complete failure to recognise, learn from, and come to terms with reality.

It is often difficult to verify the existence of an ego defence mechanism, but a person's denial in the face of hard evidence to the contrary can easily be spotted by almost anyone else. Many more problems arise in the absence of such hard evidence, not only because the denial can no longer be spotted, but also because it can be imagined or invented by others. Indeed, the charge of denial can be levied at anything and everything that a person can say or do that runs contrary to some pet theory about him, such that the pet theory can only ever be supported but never refuted. For example, if a patient undergoing psychotherapy is regarded by his psychotherapist as being in denial about his sexual orientation, then both disagreeing with the psychotherapist and having a string of heterosexual relationships can be taken to confirm his supposed homosexuality: 'You're only saying this because you're in denial… You only did that because you're in denial.' As a result, the patient cannot possibly prove his heterosexuality to the psychotherapist, and might even come to believe that the psychotherapist is in fact correct.

An ego defence that is closely related to denial is negative hallucination, which is the unconscious failure to perceive uncomfortable sensory stimuli, for instance, the failure to see something that is clearly visible, hear something that is clearly audible, or feel something – such as crushing chest pain – that should clearly be felt. Thus, a common experience in conversation or in a social setting is for a person to 'edit out' a pertinent remark that attacks his construct of the self, of another, or of reality, and then to carry on listening and interacting as if the remark had never been uttered. To be able to hear the unbearable is one of the many challenges of the good listener.

> events that took place

2. Repression

Repression can be thought of as 'motivated forgetting': the active but unconscious 'forgetting' of unacceptable drives, emotions, ideas, or memories. Unsurprisingly, repression is often confused with denial: whereas denial relates to external stimuli, repression relates to internal, that is, mental, stimuli. Nonetheless, denial and repression often work together and may, as in the following case, be difficult to disentangle from each other.

In the immediate aftermath of the 9/11 attacks on the Twin Towers, an estimated 200 people jumped to their deaths to avoid being killed in the smoking fires. Some might have lost their footing, others been pushed out by an explosive force, but it remains likely that many chose to jump to escape from the suffocating smoke and dust, the blistering flames, and the steel-bending heat. These so-called 'jumpers' chose the manner of their death (in so far as they had a choice, given their horrific circumstances), and many people see that choice as a heroic act of defiance in the face of near certain death.

Some tried to make parachutes out of curtains or table cloths, only to have them ripped out of their hands as soon as they had started falling. Depending on body position, the speed of their fall from a height of 110 storeys, that is, more than 1300ft, might have reached up to 200mph; upon hitting the ground, they stood absolutely no chance of surviving, with their bodies being not so much broken as obliterated. Several years on, there has been little interest in uncovering the identities of these 200 or so jumpers; the official account remains that nobody jumped, and that all 2,753 victims in the Twin Towers died from 'blunt impact' injuries. On the first anniversary of the tragedy, a bronze sculpture by Eric Fischl, *Tumbling Woman* (Figure 1), was unveiled in Rockefeller Center. The sculpture depicted a naked woman with her arms and legs flailing above her head, and was accompanied by a short poem by the artist,

> *We watched,*
> *disbelieving and helpless,*
> *on that savage day.*
> *People we love*
> *began falling,*
> *helpless and in disbelief.*

The sculpture gave rise to so much protest that, within a matter of only days, it had to be draped in cloth and surrounded by a curtain and then finally removed. Fischl released a statement defending his intent, 'The sculpture was not meant to hurt anybody,' he said. 'It was a sincere expression of deepest sympathy of the vulnerability of the human condition. Both specifically towards the victims of September 11 and towards humanity in general.' In a subsequent interview with the poet Ilka Scobie, Fischl said, 'the thing around 9/11 is that it was this horrific event that killed 3,000 people but there were no bodies. If you remember all the passion was centred on architecture to replace the Towers. To secure the footprints of the Tower. It had nothing to do with human tragedy because it was too painful. So I think that the Tumbling Woman reminded people that it was a human tragedy.'

Figure 1: *Tumbling Woman* by Eric Fischl. Bronze. Photograph by Ralph Gibson.

Freud thought of repression as the basic ego defence, since it is only when repression is fragile or failing that other ego defences come into play in a bid to reinforce and rescue it. Put differently, repression is an essential component or building block of the other ego defences. Take, for example, distortion, another common ego defence: a person who has been beaten black and blue by his father no longer remembers these traumatic events (ego defence of repression, specifically, memory repression), and instead sees his father as a gentle and loving man (ego defence of distortion). In this case, there is a clear sense of the distortion not only building upon but also supporting and reinforcing the repression.

Although repressed material is unconscious, it is no less present and can (and usually does) resurface in strange and disturbing forms. The inability to process and come to terms with repressed material can lead not only to a lack of insight and understanding – as, for example, in the case of the person who thinks that his abusive father is a gentle and loving man – but also to a range of psychological problems such as difficulty concentrating, irritability, anxiety, insomnia, nightmares, and depression, and to maladaptive and destructive patterns of behaviour such as anger and aggression in the face of reminders (such as *Tumbling Woman*) of the repressed material, the unconscious sabotaging of relationships with a potential for trust and intimacy, and, more generally, the entire gamut of ego defences and associated behaviours contained within the covers of this book.

In *Studies on Hysteria* (1895), Freud and his colleague Josef Breuer first formulated the theory that neuroses[2] have their origins in deeply traumatic and consequently repressed experiences. Treatment, they argued, requires the patient to recall these repressed experiences into consciousness and to confront them once and for all, leading to a sudden and dramatic outpouring of emotion (catharsis) and the attainment of insight. This can be achieved through the methods of free association and dream interpretation, with a relative lack of direct involvement by the psychoanalyst so as to encourage the patient to project his thoughts and feelings onto him, a process called transference (Chapter 34). In the course of the psychoanalytic process, the patient is likely to display 'resistance' in the form of changing the topic, blanking out, falling asleep, coming late, or missing appointments; such behaviour merely suggests that he is close to recalling repressed material but, for the moment, afraid of doing so. Unfortunately, things are rarely so plain sailing. One complication of the psychoanalytic process and of many

---

2 An old-fashioned term that basically describes the various forms in which repressed material can resurface such as difficulty concentrating, irritability, anxiety, etc.

other psychotherapeutic processes[3] is that they can incite the patient to confabulate false memories, for example, false memories of physical or sexual abuse in childhood. Given the grave implications that such false memories can have both for the patient and for other people, psychotherapists need to be especially sensitive to any autosuggestion on their part.

Suppression is similar to repression but with one crucial difference, namely, that the 'forgetting' is conscious rather than unconscious. Thus, suppression is the conscious and often rational decision to put an uncomfortable (although not totally unacceptable) stimulus to one side, either so as to deal with it at a later time or to abandon it altogether on the grounds that it is not worth dealing with. Being as it is a conscious operation, suppression is not – strictly speaking – a form of self-deception, but rather the conscious analogue of repression. Needless to say, suppression is a much more

---

3   People often confuse psychotherapy, psychoanalysis, psychology, and psychiatry. (1) A psychotherapist is any person trained in delivering specialized talking treatments – commonly a clinical psychologist or a psychiatrist. (2) A psychoanalyst is a type of psychotherapist trained in delivering specialized talking treatments based on psychoanalytic principles pioneered by Freud and others, including Alfred Adler, Carl Jung, and Melanie Klein. (3) A clinical psychologist has expertise of human experience and behaviour; he may spend a lot of time listening to and trying to understand a patient and his relatives and carers, and may deliver specialized talking treatments such as cognitive-behavioural therapy (CBT) and family therapy. (4) A psychiatrist is a medical doctor specialized in diagnosing and treating mental disorders such as schizophrenia, bipolar affective disorder, and depression.

mature operation than repression, and, as with all conscious operations, tends to favour more positive outcomes. Take this example. A couple of friends who are holidaying with a number of other people have an argument and lose their tempers; the next day, they put their differences to one side and behave as though nothing had happened so as not to cast a cloud over the group and ruin the holiday. That day they share some good times and special moments, and by the evening it has become safe enough to discuss the argument and put it behind them. By dealing with their argument like this, they have deepened rather than undermined their friendship.

3. Anger

Anger, as in the case of *Tumbling Woman*, is a common reaction to being reminded of repressed material, and it is high time to analyse and hopefully exorcize this important and potentially destructive emotion. Plato, who is often thought of as the first philosopher, does not discuss anger in any depth, and tends to bring it up only in the context of pleasure and pain. In the *Philebus*, he says that good people delight in true or good pleasures whereas bad people delight in false or bad pleasures, and that the same goes for pain, fear, anger, and the like – thereby implying that there can be such a thing as true or good anger. Later on, he says that pleasures of the mind may be mixed with pain, as in anger or envy or love, or the mixed feelings of the spectator of tragedy or of the greater drama of life – this time implying that anger can be pleasurable as well as painful. In the *Timaeus*, he lists five terrible affections of the mortal soul: pleasure, the inciter of evil; pain, which deters from good; rashness and fear, foolish counsellors; anger, hard to appease; and hope, easily led astray. The gods, he says, mingled these affections with irrational sense and all-daring love, and so created man.

Unlike Plato, Aristotle – who studied and taught in Plato's Academy for some 20 years – discusses anger at great length. In Book 2 of the *Nicomachean Ethics*, he appears to agree with Plato by saying that a good-tempered person can sometimes get angry, but only as he ought to. A good-tempered person, he continues, might get angry too soon or not enough, yet still be praised for being good-tempered; it is only if he deviates more widely from the mean with respect to anger that he becomes blameworthy, either 'irascible' at one extreme or 'lacking in spirit' at the other. Aristotle then, famously, tells us,

> *For in everything it is no easy task to find the middle ... anyone can get angry – that is easy – or give or spend money; but to do this to the right person, to the right extent, at the right time, with the right motive, and in the right way, that is not for everyone, nor is it easy; wherefore goodness is both rare and laudable and noble.*[4]

Aristotle also agrees with Plato that anger involves mixed feelings of pleasure and pain. In Book 2 of the *Rhetoric*, in discussing the emotions, he defines anger as an impulse,

---

4   Translated by WD Ross.

accompanied by pain, to a conspicuous revenge for a conspicuous slight that has been directed either at the person himself or at his friends; he then adds that anger is also attended by a certain pleasure that arises from the expectation of revenge. A person is slighted out of one of three things, contempt, spite, and insolence; in either case, the slight betrays the offender's feeling that the slighted person is obviously of no importance. The slighted person may or may not get angry, but he is more likely to get angry if he is in distress – for example, in poverty or in love – or if he feels insecure about the subject of the slight. On the other hand, he is less likely to get angry if the slight is involuntary, unintentional, or itself provoked by anger, or if the offender apologises or humbles himself before him and behaves like his inferior. Even dogs, Aristotle tells us, do not bite sitting people. The slighted person is also less likely to get angry if the offender has done him more kindnesses than he has returned, or reverences him, or is feared and respected by him. Once provoked, anger is calmed by: the feeling that the slight is deserved, the passage of time, the exaction of revenge, the suffering of the offender, or being spent on someone or other. Thus, although angrier at Ergophilius than at Callisthenes, the people acquitted Ergophilius because they had already condemned Callisthenes to death.[5]

---

5   Callisthenes concluded a premature peace with Perdiccas, king of
     Macedonia, while Ergophilus failed in an attack on Cotys, king of
     Thrace.

There is clearly a sense in which Plato and Aristotle are correct in speaking of such a thing as a good or right anger. Anger can serve a number of useful, even vital, functions. It can put an end to a bodily, emotional, or social threat, or – failing that – it can mobilise mental and physical resources for defensive or corrective action. If judiciously exercised, it can enable a person to signal confidence and high social status, compete for rank and position, strengthen bargaining positions, ensure that contracts and promises are fulfilled, and even inspire desirable feelings such as respect and sympathy. A person who is able to express or exercise anger judiciously may feel better about himself, more in control, more optimistic, and more prone to the sort of risk-taking that promotes successful outcomes. On the other hand, anger, and in particular uncontrolled anger, can lead to loss of perspective and judgement, impulsive and irrational behaviour that is harmful both to the self and to others, and loss of face, sympathy, and social credibility. Thus, it appears that the sort of anger that is justified, controlled, strategic, and potentially adaptive ought to be demarcated from and contrasted with a second type of anger (let us call it 'rage') that is inappropriate, unjustified, unprocessed, irrational, undifferentiated, and uncontrolled. It goes without saying that the anger that arises from being reminded of repressed material is of this latter, insightless and destructive kind. The function of rage is simply to protect the ego: it causes pain of one kind to detract from pain of another, and is attended by very little pleasure if any at all. These various distinctions are summarized in the Table 1.

Table 1: Analysis of anger

	Justified anger	**Unjustified anger (rage)**
Cause	• Being slighted	• Being reminded of repressed material
Features	• Justified • Controlled • Strategic • Useful	• Inappropriate • Unjustified • Unprocessed • Irrational • Insightless • Uncontrolled • Destructive
Effects	• Puts an end to a threat • Mobilizes resources for corrective action • Strengthens bargaining positions • Ensures that contracts and promises are fulfilled • Promotes risk taking • Signals confidence and high social status • Consolidates social rank and position • Inspires respect and sympathy • Improves self-image • Can produce pleasure	• Signals insecurity • Damages interests • Damages relationships • Detrimental to self-image • Produces unalloyed pain

Another, related, idea is this. Anger, and particularly rage, strengthens correspondence bias, that is, the tendency to attribute observed behaviours to dispositional or personality-related factors[6]. For instance, if I forgot to do the dishes, I reason that this is because I suddenly felt very tired (situational factor), whereas if Emma forgot to do the dishes, I reason that this is because she is lazy (dispositional factor). More fundamentally, anger reinforces the illusion that people exercise a high degree of free will, whereas in actual fact most of a person's actions and the neurological activity that they correspond to are determined by past events and the cumulative effects of those past events on that person's patterns of thinking[7]. It follows that the only person who can truly deserve anger is the one who acted freely, that is, the one who spited us freely and therefore probably rightly! This does not mean that anger is not justified in other cases, as a display of anger – even if undeserved – can still serve a benevolent strategic purpose. But if all that is ever required is a strategic display of anger, then true anger that involves real pain and destruction is entirely superfluous, its presence only serving to betray … a certain lack of understanding.

---

6   Another term for correspondence bias is 'fundamental attribution error'.

7   See Chapter 2 of *The Art of Failure* for the full argument.

4. Dissociation

The ego defence of 'isolation of affect' involves a dissociation of thoughts and feelings, with the feelings (the affect) then removed from conscious attention to leave only the thoughts. It can be evidenced, for example, in people who refer to an emotionally loaded event or situation in a casual, matter-of-fact, or otherwise dispassionate way. Isolation of affect can be useful in certain situations, for example, in providing the distance and objectivity that a physician needs to make the right or best decisions about the care of his patients; at the same time, too much detachment neither makes for a good physician, and detachment is best if it is conscious and appropriate rather than rigid and defensive.

Much more dramatic – and correspondingly less common – forms of dissociation might occur after a traumatic event, and result in a disruption of the normally integrated functions of consciousness, memory, identity, and perception of the environment. According to modern classifications of mental disorders, such dissociative disorders, as they are called, may involve overlapping conditions such as (1) amnesia, (2) fugue, (3) possession trance, and (4) stupor. (1) In dissociative amnesia, the person suffers a loss of memory, most commonly for the period surrounding the traumatic event. Amnesia as a method of self-preservation has been recognized since at least the first century; in his *Natural History*, Pliny the Elder remarked that, 'Nothing whatever, in man, is of so frail a nature as the memory; for it is affected by disease, by injuries, and even by fright; being sometimes partially lost, and at other times entirely so.' (2) In dissociative fugue, the traumatic event prompts the person to embark on an unexpected journey that may last for up to several months. During this journey, there is memory loss and confusion about personal identity or assumption of another identity. Once the fugue ends, the memory of the journey is usually lost. (3) In possession trance, the person reacts to the traumatic event by entering a dissociative (trance) state in which his identity is replaced by that of another person, animal, or inanimate object, or, more commonly, by a ghost, spirit, or deity. A trance state can be an accepted, even an exalted, expression of religious feeling, and should only be considered problematic or potentially problematic if it is not sanctioned by the person's culture or sub-culture. (4) Finally, in dissociative stupor, the person reacts to the traumatic event by becoming motionless and mute, failing to respond to stimuli such as the human voice, bright lights, or extremes of hot and cold.

The already famous and very glamorous mystery writer Agatha Christie (Figue 2) disappeared from her home in Berkshire, England, on the evening of December 3, 1926. Her mother, to whom she had been close, had died some months earlier, and her husband Colonel Archibald Christie was having an affair with one Nancy Neele. Archie made little effort to disguise this affair, and on the day that Agatha disappeared he had gone to the home of some friends in Surrey to be reunited with Nancy. Before vanishing, Agatha had written several confused notes to Archie and others: in one, she wrote that she was going on holiday to Yorkshire, but in another that she feared for her life. The following morning, Agatha's abandoned car was discovered with headlights on and bonnet up in Surrey, not far from a lake called Silent Pool in which she had drowned one of her fictional characters. Inside the green Morris Cowley, she had left her fur coat, a suitcase with her belongings, and an expired driver's license. Fearing the obvious, the police dredged the lake, organised as many as 15,000 volunteers to beat the surrounding countryside, and even (for the first time in England for a missing person) flew aeroplanes overhead – but all without any trace of the famous writer.

In fact, Agatha had checked into a health spa in Harrogate, Yorkshire, not under her own name but – significantly – under that of 'Teresa Neele'. Her disappearance soon made the national headlines; several people at the spa thought to have recognised her, but she kept on telling them that she was merely a bereaved mother from Cape Town. Only when, on December 14, the police brought Archie up to Harrogate could Agatha be reliably and conclusively identified. As Archie entered the spa, Agatha simply said, 'Fancy, my brother has just arrived.' Agatha never discussed this perplexing episode and also excluded it from her biography. Perhaps she contrived it as a publicity stunt, maybe as a cry of despair or act of revenge, but a dissociative fugue is an equally likely explanation, and also

Figure 2: Agatha Christie. 'Understand this, I mean to arrive at the truth. The truth, however ugly in itself, is always curious and beautiful to seekers after it.' – Hercule Poirot, *The Murder of Roger Ackroyd* (1926).

the one upheld by her then physicians. In any case, it should be borne in mind that, just like dissociative fugue, denial, or repression, fame and revenge also function as ego defences. In Agatha's own words, 'Most successes are unhappy. That's why they are successes – they have to reassure themselves about themselves by achieving something that the world will notice … The happy people are failures because they are on such good terms with themselves that they don't give a damn.'

There can be no doubt that denial is an important component of any dissociative disorder, whether fugue, amnesia, trance, or stupor. Although dissociative disorders are commonly described as a 'compartmentalization of experience', in many cases they can also be thought of as nothing more than an extreme form of denial. As our exercise in defining and distinguishing the various ego defences has already begun to reveal, ego defences tend to involve a great deal of overlap. To avoid getting tied in knots about the definitional niceties of one or another particular ego defence, it can be helpful to remember that each ego defence, rather than existing in splendid isolation, simply emphasizes a certain aspect of psychological functioning, and that self-deception often involves not one but several overlapping and mutually reinforcing ego defences.

5. Intellectualization

Isolation of affect – the dissociation of thoughts and feelings, with the feelings then removed from conscious attention to leave only the thoughts – is closely related to intellectualization. In intellectualization, the uncomfortable feelings associated with a problem are kept out of consciousness by thinking about the problem in cold, abstract, and esoteric terms. First example: I once received a phone call from a junior doctor in psychiatry in which he described a recent in-patient admission as 'a 47-year old mother of two *who attempted to cessate her life as a result of being diagnosed with a metastatic mitotic lesion*'. A formulation such as '...who tried to kill herself after being told that she is dying of cancer' would have been much better English, but would also have been all too effective at evoking the full horror of this poor lady's predicament.

Second example: An ambitious medical student once asked me whether she should take up a career in academic medicine, despite (or so it seemed) having already made up her mind on the matter. I raised some arguments in favour and then some arguments against such a move, in particular that only a very small number of people engaged in medical research ever make a significant discovery. As she did not seem to be taking this argument on board, I asked her to name just one major breakthrough from the past 50 years in the life of a particular top-rated medical research department. Instead of accepting that the department had not made a single major breakthrough in 50 years of publishing one academic paper after another, she resorted to questioning the definition of a breakthrough and then the value of making one.

Third example: After being discharged from hospital, a middle-aged man who had almost died from a heart attack spent several hours a day on his computer researching the various risk factors for cardiovascular disease. He typed out long essays on each of these risk factors, printed them out, and filed them in a large binder with colour-coded dividers. After having done all this, he became preoccupied with the vitamin and mineral contents in various kinds of food, and devised a strict dietary regimen to ensure that he took in the recommended amounts of each and every micronutrient. Despite living on a shoestring budget, he spent several hundred pounds on a high-end steamer on the basis that it could preserve vitamins through the cooking process. Although he expended an inordinate amount of effort, time, and money on his persnickety diet, he did not even once consider cutting back on his far, far more noxious smoking habit.

The focus on abstract notions and trivial footnotes often belies a sort of 'flight into reason'; the emotionally loaded event or situation is thought of in terms of an interesting problem or puzzle, without any appreciation for its emotional content or personal implications. Instead of coming to terms with the problem, the person may split hairs over definitions; question reasonable assumptions, facts, and arguments; and preoccupy himself with abstruse minutiae. By failing to perceive the bigger picture, he also fails to reach the appropriate conclusion or conclusions, which, as with our medical student or heart attack victim, may hit him very hard come five, ten, or fifty years' time. Intellectualization can also underlie a number of logical fallacies and rhetorical blind alleys, such as raising irrelevant or trivial counter-arguments, rejecting an argument on the basis of an inaccurate example or exceptional case, using exact numbers for inexact or abstract notions, and 'blinding with science'. In short, the person appears to be engaging with, and even to be excited by, a certain problem, but without ever truly getting to the bottom of it.

Isolation of affect and intellectualization should be distinguished from plain and simple isolation, which can be thought of as the inverse of intellectualization. Whereas intellectualization involves repressing the emotion but not the thought, isolation involves repressing the thought but not the emotion. The person feels a strong emotion, often breaking down in tears, but is entirely unable to point to its cause. After regaining his composure, he is likely to repress the emotion or its memory until – if he should be so lucky – it returns with a vengeance several years later.

6. Rationalization

Intellectualization is easy to confuse with rationalization. Whereas intellectualization is to use a barrage of intellectual activity to cover up an uncomfortable feeling, rationalization is to use feeble but seemingly plausible arguments either to justify something that is difficult to accept or to make it seem 'not so bad after all'. First example: A person who has been rejected by a love interest convinces himself that she rejected him because she did not share in his ideal of happiness, and, furthermore, that the rejection is a blessing in disguise in that it has freed him to find a more suitable partner. The first rationalization (that his love interest rejected him because they did not share in the same ideal of happiness) is a case of justifying something that is difficult to accept, sometimes referred to as 'sour grapes'. The second rationalization (that the rejection has freed him to find a more suitable partner) is a case of making it seem 'not so bad after all', also referred to as 'sweet lemons'.

Second example: A teenager who fails to secure a place at Cambridge University tells herself that one of the interviewers on the interviewing panel was sexist (sour grapes), and, furthermore, that taking a gap year to reapply is going to give her a precious opportunity to travel and see the world (sweet lemons). The teenager uses these rationalizations to reduce the psychological discomfort of holding contradictory beliefs or thoughts ('cognitions'), on the one hand the cognition that she is intelligent enough to get into Cambridge University, and on the other hand the cognition that she failed to do so. She could have reduced this so-called 'cognitive dissonance' by adapting her self-image ('I am perhaps not so intelligent as I thought'), but finds it less challenging to undermine, that is, to rationalize, the inconsistent cognition of her rejection by Cambridge University.

Third example: A striking instance of cognitive dissonance and rationalization can be found in Leon Festinger's book of 1956, *When Prophecy Fails*, in which he discusses his experience of infiltrating a UFO doomsday cult the leader of which had recently prophesised the end of the world. When the end of the world (rather predictably) failed to materialise, most of the cult's members dealt with the cognitive dissonance that arose from the cognitions 'the leader prophesized that the world is going to end' and 'the world did not end' *not* by abandoning the cult or its leader, as might be expected, but by introducing the rationalization that the world had been saved by the strength of their faith.

Fourth example: Smokers typically experience a high level of cognitive dissonance with respect to their smoking. To decrease this tension, they might quit cigarettes, or deny the evidence that links smoking to life-threatening conditions such as chronic obstructive pulmonary disease (COPD) and lung cancer, or rationalize their smoking so as to make it compatible with competing cognitions such as 'I want to live a long and healthy life' and 'I am a reasonable person who makes good decisions'. For example, they might tell themselves that smoking is their only way of coping, that there is nothing else to do, that there is no point in living if life cannot be enjoyed, that only heavy smokers are at risk of COPD and lung cancer, that everyone must die from something or other, or that everyone must die some day. The first three are instances of sour grapes, the last three of sweet lemons.

For the story, 'sour grapes' derives from one of the fables attributed to Aesop, *The Fox and the Grapes*.

> *On one hot summer's day a Fox was strolling through an orchard till he came to a bunch of Grapes just ripening on a vine which had been trained over a lofty branch. 'Just the thing to quench my thirst', quoth he. Drawing back a few paces, he took a run and a jump, and just missed the branch. Turning round with a One, Two, Three, he jumped up, but with no greater success.*

> *Again and again he tried after the tempting morsel, but at last had to give it up, and walked away with his nose in their air, saying: 'I am sure they are sour.'*

In the case of Aesop's fox, the cognitive dissonance arises from the cognitions 'I am an agile and nimble fox' and 'I can't reach the grapes on the branch', and the rationalization, which is a form of 'sour grapes', is 'I am sure the grapes are sour'. Had the fox chosen to use 'sweet lemons' instead of 'sour grapes', he might have said something like, 'In any case, there are far juicier grapes in the farmer's orchard.'

Rationalization is used to great comic effect in *Candide: Or, Optimism*, the satirical masterpiece of the 18th century Enlightenment thinker Voltaire. The novella is an attack on Leibniz's philosophy that our world is the best of all possible worlds, a philosophy that is very much taken to heart by Candide's old tutor Professor Pangloss, who stubbornly persists in rationalizing a succession of tragic events to keep them in line with this being the best of all possible worlds. In Chapter 4, Candide chances upon Pangloss in the form of a beggar who, having contracted the venereal disease of syphilis, is covered in scabs and coughing violently. Upon discovering Pangloss in such a debased condition, Candide 'inquires into the cause and effect, as well as into the sufficing reason that had reduced [him] to so miserable a condition'.

P: *Alas ... it was love; love, the comfort of the human species; love, the preserver of the universe; the soul of all sensible beings; love! tender love!*

C: *Alas ... I have had some knowledge of love myself, this sovereign of hearts, this soul of souls; yet it never cost me more than a kiss and twenty kicks on the backside. But how could this beautiful cause produce in you so hideous an effect? (...)*

P: *Oh my dear Candide, you must remember Pacquette, that pretty wench, who waited on our noble Baroness; in her arms I tasted the pleasures of Paradise, which produced these Hell torments with which you see me devoured. She was infected with an ailment, and perhaps has since died of it; she received this present of a learned Franciscan, who derived it from the fountainhead; he was indebted for it to an old countess, who had it of a captain of horse, who had it of a marchioness, who had it of a page, the page had it of a Jesuit, who, during his novitiate, had it in a direct line from one of the fellow adventurers of Christopher Columbus...*

C: *O sage Pangloss ... what a strange genealogy is this! Is not the devil the root of it?*

P: *Not at all ... it was a thing unavoidable, a necessary ingredient in the best of worlds; for if Columbus had not caught in an island in America this disease, which contaminates the source of generation, and frequently impedes propagation itself, and is evidently opposed to the great end of nature, we should have had neither chocolate nor cochineal...*

7. Positive illusions

Most people see themselves in a much more positive light than others do them, and possess an unduly rose-tinted perspective on their attributes, circumstances, and possibilities. Such positive illusions, as they are called, are of three broad kinds, an inflated sense of one's qualities and abilities, an illusion of control over things that are mostly or entirely out of one's control, and an unrealistic optimism about the future. For example, most people think that they are a better than average driver, citizen, or parent, collectively implying that the average driver, citizen, or parent is in fact not at all average, which is obviously a statistical impossibility.

A couple on the verge of getting married is likely to over-estimate the odds of having a sunny honeymoon or a gifted child but underestimate the odds of having a miscarriage, falling ill, or getting divorced. Positive illusions may confer certain advantages such as an ability to take risks, see through major undertakings, and cope with traumatic events. In the longer term, however, the loss of perspective and poor judgement that come from undue self-regard and false hope are likely to lead to failure and disappointment, not to mention the emotional and behavioural problems (such as anger, anxiety, and so on) that can be associated with a defended position.

Of particular note is that positive illusions are more prevalent in Occidental and Occidentalized cultures. In East Asian cultures, for example, people do not tend to self-enhance and may even be self-effacing. Culture can influence not just ego defences used, but also presentation and reaction to mental disorder, and, indeed, the content of dreams and psychotic experiences. For example, in many traditional societies, 'depression' is more frequently experienced as a physical symptom such as fatigue, headache, or chest pain than as depressed mood, and some 'mental disorders' such as brief reactive psychosis and dissociative trance may be considered as normal and even exalted states.

At the same time, people from traditional societies might display culture-specific patterns of aberrant behaviour and troubling experience that are not easily accommodated by European and American psychiatric classifications, and that have imperialistically been called 'culture-bound syndromes'. An example of a culture-bound syndrome is koro, which is seen in Indian and South Asian men and involves sudden and intense fear of the penis retracting into the body and causing death. Koro may represent a reaction to sexual guilt, with some afflicted men going so far as to fasten their penis to posts or pieces of furniture so as to prevent their deadly retraction. Other examples of culture-bound syndromes are susto, which is seen in Latin American populations and involves the belief that the soul has left the body as a result of receiving a sudden fright[8], and, indeed, anorexia nervosa and bulimia nervosa, which, although included in the European and American psychiatric classifications, are only ever seen in Occidental or Occidentalized populations.

Positive illusions are more prevalent not only in Occidental and Occidentalized cultures, but also in unskilled people. The explanation for this is thought to be that, in contrast to unskilled people, highly skilled people tend to assume – albeit falsely – that those around them enjoy a similar level of competence to them. This so-called Dunning-Kruger effect is neatly encapsulated in a short fragment from the introduction to Darwin's *Descent of Man*: '…ignorance more frequently begets confidence than does knowledge…' And of course it may also and simply be that, compared to highly skilled people, unskilled people are far more dependent on positive illusions for their self-esteem.

---

8   Another name for susto is *Perdida de la sombra*, which translates
     from the Spanish as 'loss of the shadow'. The loss of the soul in susto is
     thought to leave the body exposed and vulnerable to disease.

In contrast to most, people with depression are prone to a number of cognitive biases or distortions that might be thought of as 'negative illusions'. Three types of cognitive distortion that occur in depression are arbitrary inference, overgeneralization, and selective abstraction. (1) Arbitrary inference is reaching a conclusion in the absence of supportive evidence, for example – not uncommon in severe depression – 'The whole world hates me.' (2) Overgeneralization is similar to arbitrary inference, but rather than reaching a conclusion in the absence of supportive evidence, the person reaches a conclusion on the basis of little more than flimsy, anecdotal evidence, often a single incident, as in, 'My son did not come to see me today – the whole world hates me.' (3) Selective abstraction is focusing on a single negative event or condition to the exclusion of other, more positive ones. For instance, a person may be preoccupied by the fact the he is not currently in a relationship, but neglect the fact that, unlike many other people, he has a supportive family and many good friends. Other types of cognitive distortion commonly seen in depression include dichotomous thinking, personalization, magnification, minimization, and catastrophic thinking. The topic of depression is revisited in Chapter 9.

8. The manic defence

The manic defence joins positive illusions and the sweet lemons variety of rationalization to complete the 'half-full rather than half-empty' collection of ego defences. The manic defence, which I also discussed at great length and in similar terms in *The Art of Failure* (2010), refers to the tendency, when presented with uncomfortable thoughts or feelings, to distract the conscious mind either with a flurry of activity or with the opposite thoughts or feelings. A general example of the manic defence is the person who spends all of his time rushing around from one task to the next, and unable to tolerate even short periods of inactivity. For this person, even leisure time consists in a series of discrete programmed activities that he needs to submit to in order to tick off from an actual or mental list. One needs only observe the expression on his face as he ploughs through yet another family outing, cultural event, or gruelling exercise routine to realise that his aim in life is not so much to live in the present moment as it is to work down his never-ending list. If one asks him how he is doing, he is most likely to respond with an artificial smile and a robotic response along the lines of, 'Fine, thank you – very busy of course!' In many cases, he is not fine at all, but confused, exhausted, and fundamentally unhappy.

Other, more specific, examples of the manic defence include the socialite who attends one event after another, the small and dependent boy who charges around declaiming that he is Superman, and the sexually inadequate adolescent who laughs 'like a maniac' at the slightest intimation of sex. It is important to distinguish this sort of 'manic laughter' from the more mature laughter that arises from suddenly revealing or emphasizing the ridiculous or absurd aspects of an anxiety-provoking person, event, or situation. Such mature laughter enables a person to see a problem in a more accurate and less threatening context, and so to diffuse the anxiety that it gives rise to. All that is required to make a person laugh is to tell him the truth in the guise of a joke or a tease; drop the pretence, however, and the effect is entirely different. In short, laughter can be used either to reveal the truth or – as in the case of the manic defence – to conceal it or to block it out.

Indeed, the essence of the manic defence is to prevent feelings of helplessness and despair from entering the conscious mind by occupying it with opposite feelings of euphoria, purposeful activity, and omnipotent control. This is no doubt why people feel driven not only to mark but also to *celebrate* such depressing milestones as entering the workforce (graduation), getting ever older (birthdays, New Year), and even, more recently, death and dying (Halloween) – laughing when they should be crying and crying when they should be laughing. The manic defence may also take on more subtle forms, such as creating a commotion over something trivial; filling every 'spare moment' with reading, study, or on the phone to a friend; spending several months preparing for Christmas or some civic or sporting event; seeking out status or celebrity so as to be a 'somebody' rather than a 'nobody'; entering into baseless friendships and relationships; even, sometimes, getting married and having children.

In Virginia Woolf's novel of 1925, *Mrs Dalloway*, one of several ways in which Clarissa Dalloway prevents herself from thinking about her life is by planning unneeded events and then preoccupying herself with their prerequisites – 'always giving parties to cover the silence'. Everyone uses the manic defence, but some people use it to such an extent that they find it difficult to cope with even short periods of unstructured time, such as holidays, weekends, and long-distance travel, which at least explains why airport shops are so profitable. In sum, it is not that the manically defended person is happy – not at all, in fact – but that he does not know how to be sad. As the 19th century writer Oscar Wilde (Figure 3) put it in his essay, *The Critic as Artist: With Some Remarks on the Importance of Doing Nothing*, 'To do nothing at all is the most

Figure 3: Oscar Wilde. Photograph by Napoleon Sarony (1882).
'We are dominated by the fanatic, whose worst vice is his sincerity.
Anything approaching to the free play of the mind is practically
unknown amongst us. People cry out against the sinner, yet it is not
the sinful, but the stupid, who are our shame. There is no sin except
stupidity.'

difficult thing in the world, the most difficult and the most intellectual.'

Like positive illusions, the manic defence is particularly prevalent in Occidental and Occidentalized societies. One of the central tenets of the Western worldview is that one should always be engaged in some kind of outward task; in contrast, most people living in a country such as Kenya in Africa do not share in this idea that it is somehow noble or worthwhile to spend all of one's time rushing around from one task to the next. When Westerners go to Kenya and behave as they do back home, they are met with peels of laughter and cries of *Mzungu*, which is Swahili for 'Westerner'. The literal translation of *Mzungu* is 'one who moves around', 'to go round and round', or 'to turn around in circles'.

Sometimes, however, a life situation can become so unfulfilling or untenable that the manic defence no longer suffices to block out negative feelings, and the person has no real choice but to switch and to adopt the depressive position. Put differently, a person adopts the depressive position if the gap between his current life situation and his ideal life situation becomes so large that it can no longer be carpeted over. His goals seem far out of reach and he can no longer envisage a future. As in Psalm 41, *abyssus abyssum invocat* – 'hell brings forth hell', or, in an alternative translation, 'the deep calls onto the deep'.

9. Depression

We are healed of a suffering only by experiencing it to the full.

– Marcel Proust, *In Search of Lost Time*

Most people think of depression as a mental disorder, that is, a biological illness of the brain. Here I argue that the concept of depression as a mental disorder has been unhelpfully overextended to include all manner of human suffering. I further argue that 'depression' can be good for us – an idea that I first visited in *The Meaning of Madness* (2008).

Let us begin by thinking very broadly about the concept of depression. There are important geographical variations in the prevalence of depression, and these can in large part be accounted for by socio-cultural rather than biological factors. In traditional societies, human distress is more likely to be seen as an indicator of the need to address important life problems rather than as a mental disorder requiring professional treatment. For this reason, the diagnosis of depression is correspondingly less common. Some linguistic communities do not have a word or even a concept for 'depression', and many people from traditional societies with what may be construed as depression present with physical complaints such as fatigue, headache, or chest pain rather than with psychological complaints. Thus, Punjabi women who have recently immigrated to the UK and given birth find it baffling that a health visitor should pop round to ask them if they are depressed. Not only had they never considered the possibility that giving birth could be anything other than a joyous event, but they do not even have a word with which to translate the concept of 'depression' into Punjabi.

In modern societies such as the UK and the USA, people talk about depression more readily and more easily. As a result, they are more likely to interpret their distress in terms of depression, and less likely to fear being stigmatized if they seek out a diagnosis of the illness. At the same time, groups with vested interests such as pharmaceutical companies and mental health experts promote the notion of saccharine happiness as a natural, default state, and of human distress as a mental disorder. The concept of depression as a mental disorder may be useful for the more severe and intractable cases treated by hospital psychiatrists, but probably not for the majority of cases, which, for the most part, are mild and short-lived, and easily interpreted in terms of life circumstances, human nature, or the human condition.

Another (non-mutually exclusive) explanation for the important geographical variations in the prevalence of depression may lie in the nature of modern societies, which have become increasingly individualistic and divorced from traditional values. For many people living in our society, life can seem both suffocating and far removed, lonely even and especially among the multitudes, and not only meaningless but absurd. By encoding their distress in terms of a mental disorder, our society may be subtly implying that the problem lies not with itself but with them, fragile and failing individuals that they are. Of course, many people prefer to buy into this reductive, physicalist explanation than to confront their existential angst, an ego defence called reification (Chapter 15). However, thinking of unhappiness in terms of an illness or chemical imbalance can be counterproductive, as it can prevent people from identifying and addressing the important psychological or life problems that are at the root of their distress.

All this is not to say that the concept of depression as a mental disorder is bogus, but only that the diagnosis of depression has been over-extended to include far more than just depression the mental disorder. If, like the majority of medical conditions, depression could be defined and diagnosed according to its aetiology or pathology – that is, cause or effect – such a state of affairs could not have arisen. Unfortunately, depression cannot as yet be defined according to its aetiology or pathology, but only according to its clinical manifestations and symptoms. For this reason, a doctor cannot base a diagnosis of depression on any objective criterion such as a blood test or a brain scan, but only on his subjective interpretation of the nature and severity of the patient's symptoms. If some of these symptoms appear to tally with the diagnostic criteria for depression, then the doctor is able to justify a diagnosis of depression.

One important problem here is that the definition of 'depression' is circular: the concept of depression is defined according to the symptoms of depression, which are in turn defined according to the concept of depression. Thus, it is impossible to be certain that the concept of depression maps onto any distinct disease entity, particularly since a diagnosis of depression can apply to anything from mild depression to depressive psychosis and depressive stupor, and overlap with several other categories of mental disorder including dysthymia[9], adjustment disorders[10], and anxiety disorders. Indeed, one of the consequences of the 'menu of symptoms'

---

9   Dysthymia can be defined as a mild long-term depression characterized by depressive symptoms that are not sufficiently severe to warrant a diagnosis of depression.

10   Adjustment disorder can be defined as a protracted response to a significant life change or life event characterized by depressive symptoms and/or anxiety symptoms that are not sufficiently severe to warrant a diagnosis of depression but that nonetheless impair social functioning.

approach to diagnosing depression is that two people with absolutely no symptoms in common (not even depressed mood) can both end up with the same diagnosis of depression. For this reason especially, the concept of depression has been charged with being little more than a socially constructed dustbin for all manner of human suffering.

Let us grant, as the orthodoxy propounds, that every person inherits a certain complement of genes that make him more or less vulnerable to entering a state that could be diagnosed as depression (and let us henceforth refer to this state as 'the depressive position' to include both clinical depression and other states of depressed mood). A person adopts the depressive position if the amount of stress that he comes under is greater than the amount of stress that he can tolerate, given the complement of genes that he has inherited. Genes for potentially debilitating disorders gradually pass out of a population over time because affected people have, on average, fewer children than non-affected people. The fact that this has not happened for even clinical depression (which could be considered as the most debilitating extreme of a spectrum of depressed mood) suggests that the genes responsible are being maintained despite their potentially debilitating effects on a significant proportion of the population[11], and thus that they

11 Clinical depression is associated with a much higher than average suicide rate, not to mention its detrimental effects on ability to thrive, mating success, child rearing, and so on.

are conferring an important adaptive advantage. There are other instances of genes that both predispose to an illness and confer an important adaptive advantage. In sickle cell disease, for example, red blood cells assume a rigid sickle shape that restricts their passage through tiny blood vessels. This leads to a number of serious physical complications and, in traditional societies, to a radically shortened life expectancy. At the same time, carrying just one allele of the sickle cell gene ('sickle cell trait') makes it impossible for malarial parasites to reproduce into red blood cells, and so confers immunity to malaria. The fact that the gene for sickle cell anaemia is particularly common in populations from malarial regions suggests that, in evolutionary terms, a debilitating illness in the few can be a price worth paying for an important adaptive advantage in the many.

What important adaptive advantage could the depressive position be conferring? Just as physical pain has evolved to signal injury and to prevent further injury, so the depressive position may have evolved to remove us from distressing, damaging, or futile situations. The time and space and solitude that the adoption of the depressive position affords prevents us from making rash decisions, enables us to see the bigger picture, and – in the context of being a social animal – to reassess our social relationships, think about those who are significant to us, and relate to them more meaningfully and with greater understanding. Thus, the depressive position may have evolved as a signal that something is seriously wrong and needs working through and changing or, at least, understanding. Sometimes people can become so immersed in the humdrum of their everyday lives that they no longer have time to think and feel about themselves, and so lose sight of their bigger picture. The adoption of the depressive position can force them to cast off the Panglossian optimism and rose-tinted spectacles that shield them from reality, stand back at a distance, re-evaluate and prioritise their needs, and formulate a modest but realistic plan for fulfilling them.

Although the adoption of the depressive position can serve such a mundane purpose, it can also enable a person to develop a more refined perspective and deeper understanding of himself, of his life, and of life in general. From an existential standpoint, the adoption of the depressive position obliges the person to become aware of his mortality and freedom, and challenges him to exercise the latter within the framework of the former. By meeting this difficult challenge, the person is able to break out of the mould that has been imposed upon him, discover who he truly is, and, in so doing, begin to give deep meaning to his life. Indeed, many of the most creative and insightful people in society suffer or suffered from depression or a state that might have been diagnosed as depression. They include the politicians Winston Churchill and Abraham Lincoln; the poets Charles Baudelaire, Elizabeth Bishop, Hart Crane, Emily Dickinson, Sylvia Plath, and Rainer Maria

Rilke; the thinkers Michel Foucault, William James, John Stuart Mill, Isaac Newton, Friedrich Nietzsche, and Arthur Schopenhauer; and the writers Charles Dickens, William Faulkner, Graham Greene, Leo Tolstoy, Evelyn Waugh, and Tennessee Williams, among many others. To quote Marcel Proust, who also suffered from depression, 'Happiness is good for the body, but it is grief which develops the strengths of the mind.'

People in the depressive position are often stigmatised as 'failures' or 'losers'. Of course, nothing could be further from the truth. If these people are in the depressive position, it is most probably because they have tried too hard or taken on too much, so hard and so much that they have made themselves 'ill with depression'. In other words, if these people are in the depressive position, it is because their world was simply not good enough for them. They wanted more, they wanted better, and they wanted different, not just for themselves, but for all those around them. So if they are failures or losers, this is only because they set the bar far too high. They could have swept everything under the carpet and pretended, as many people do, that all is for the best in the best of possible worlds. However, unlike many people, they had the honesty and the strength to admit that something was amiss, that something was not quite right. So rather than being failures or losers, they are just the opposite: they are ambitious, truthful, and courageous. And that is precisely why they got 'ill'.

To make them believe that they are suffering from some chemical imbalance in the brain and that their recovery depends solely or even mostly on popping pills is to do them a great disfavour. It is to deny them the precious opportunity not only to identify and address important life problems, but also to develop a deeper and more nuanced appreciation of themselves and of the world around them.

Pretending everything ok → negative feeling → no personal growth / discovery → no change in situation

PART II: TRANSFORMATION

Whereas abstraction involves trying to ignore or suppress the source of the anxiety so that it no longer seems to exist, transformation involves trying to convert the anxiety into some more manageable form.

10. Displacement

Displacement is the redirection of feelings and impulses towards someone or something less threatening. The classic example of displacement is the person who has had a bad day at work. Instead of taking out his frustration on his boss or colleagues, he stores it all up until five o'clock. He then goes home, bangs the door, kicks the dog, and picks up a quarrel with his spouse.

Displacement can give rise to a chain reaction, with the victim unwittingly becoming a perpetrator. In the example above, the angry man's spouse might then hit one of their children, perhaps rationalizing her behaviour by thinking of it in terms of a punishment. The next day or month or year, the child might go to school and bully one of his classmates 'just for fun'. In his *Brief Lives*, the 17th century English biographer John Aubrey relates the following humorous anecdote about the writer and explorer Sir Walter Raleigh,

> *Mr Walt*[12] *humbled himself to his Father, and promised he would behave himself mightily mannerly. So away he went... he sate nexte to his Father and was very demure at least half dinner time. Then sayd he, I this morning, not having the feare of God before my eies, but by the instigation of the devil, went to a Whore. I was very eager of her, kissed and embraced her, and went to enjoy her, but she thrust me from her, and vowed I should not, 'For your father lay with me but an hower ago.' Sir Walt, being so strangely supprized and putt out of his countenance at so great a Table, gives his son a damned blow over the face; his son, as rude as he was, would not strike his father, but strikes over the face of the Gentleman that sate next to him, and sayed, 'Box about, 'twill come to my Father anon.'*

Displacement commonly applies to anger and frustration, but can also apply to other feelings and impulses. Thus, a person who feels lonely outside of a meaningful relationship might spend a lot of time with a placeholder or caressing and cuddling a dog or cat, and a person who is emotionally or sexually attracted to a person of the same sex but finds this completely unacceptable might 'take it out' on partners of the opposite sex. This 'taking it out' on less threatening objects often has

---

12 The son of Sir Walter.

a dual function, not only to release pent up frustration but also to reinforce the person's supposed heterosexuality, an ego defence called reaction formation (Chapter 12). A more mature response might be to convert or 'sublime' the repressed feelings and the frustration into constructive activities such as sport, study, invention, or art. Indeed, just as culture and society can be destructively displaced into the sexual impulse, so too the sexual impulse can be constructively displaced into culture and society.

Displacement also plays a role in scapegoating, in which uncomfortable feelings such as anger and guilt are displaced and projected onto another, often more vulnerable, person or group. The scapegoated person is then persecuted, providing the person doing the scapegoating not only with a conduit for his uncomfortable feelings, but also with pleasurable feelings of piety and self-righteous indignation. The creation of a villain necessarily implies that of a hero, even if both are purely fictional. A good example of a scapegoat is Marie Antoinette, Queen of Louis XVI of France, whom the French people called *L'Autre-chienne* – a pun playing on *Autrichienne* (Austrian woman) and *Autre chienne* (other bitch) – and accused of being profligate and promiscuous. When Marie Antoinette came to France to marry the then *Dauphin*[13], the country had already

---

13 The Dauphin of France or, strictly, Dauphin of Viennois, was the title carried by the heir apparent of the throne of France, and is roughly equivalent to the English Prince of Wales or Spanish Prince of Asturias.

been near bankrupted by the reckless spending of Louis XV, and the young foreign princess quickly became the target of the people's mounting ire.

Already unhappy → Deny Feelings → need an outlet → Displace → Scape goat

A more recent example of a scapegoat is the former Italian Prime Minister, Silvio Berlusconi. In November 2011, Berlusconi quickly became the fall guy for the panic engulfing the Euro Zone, with forces both within and without Italy contriving and ultimately succeeding in having his government deposed in favour of an unelected cabinet of technocrats. Berlusconi's roguish behaviour in both private and public matters could hardly have helped his case; even so, it did seem rather irrational to lay the blame for an international financial crisis onto the shoulders of a single person, albeit a hapless Prime Minister of Italy. As one commentator very succinctly put it, 'Don't turn a scoundrel into a scapegoat.'

The term 'scapegoat' usually implies a person or group, but the mechanism of scapegoating can also apply to non-human entities, whether objects, animals, or daemons. Conversely, human scapegoats are to varying degrees dehumanized, objectified, and totemized; some, such as witches in mediaeval Europe, are quite literally daemonized. The dehumanization of the scapegoat makes the scapegoating more potent and less guilt inducing, and may even lend it a sort of pre-ordained, cosmic inevitability.

The term 'scapegoat' has its origin in the Old Testament, more specifically, in Chapter 16 of the Book of Leviticus, according to which God instructed Moses and Aaron to sacrifice two goats every year. The first goat was to be killed and its blood sprinkled upon the Ark of the Covenant. The High Priest was then to lay his hands upon the head of the second goat and confess the sins of the people. Unlike the first goat, this lucky second goat was not to be killed, but to be released into the wilderness together with its burden of sin, which is why it came to be known as a, or the, scapegoat. The altar that stands in the sanctuary of every church is a symbolic remnant and reminder of this sacrificial practice, with the ultimate object of sacrifice being, of course, Jesus himself. Upon seeing Jesus for the first time, John the Baptist is said to have exclaimed, 'Behold the Lamb of God, which taketh away the sin of the world!' (John 1:29). And in Christian imagery, Jesus is often depicted as the victorious Lamb of God of the Book of Revelation, with one leg hooked around a banner with a red cross – whence the name of one of Oxford's most celebrated public houses, *The Lamb & Flag* (Figure 4). The sacrifice prescribed in the Book of Leviticus prefigures that of Jesus, who played the role of the first goat in his human crucifixion, and the role of the second goat, the scapegoat, in his divine resurrection.

An ego defence that is related to displacement, and that might be considered to be a special form of displacement, is 'turning

Figure 4: *The Lamb & Flag* public house on St Giles', Oxford, which is owned by St John's College. Profits from the pub go to fund DPhil student scholarships.

against the self", in which impulses (commonly anger) directed at another person or other people are considered frightening or unacceptable and so redirected upon the self. Turning against the self is common in people with depression, and particularly so in people with suicidal ideation. Indeed, it can be said to underlie almost every case of completed suicide.

11. Somatization

Whereas displacement (Chapter 10) entails the redirection of psychological distress towards someone or something less threatening, somatization entails its transformation or conversion into more tolerable physical symptoms. This could involve a loss of motor function in a particular group of muscles, resulting, say, in the paralysis of a limb or a side of the body (hemiplegia). Such a loss of motor function may be accompanied by a corresponding loss of sensory function. In some cases, sensory loss might be the presenting problem, particularly if it is independent of a motor loss or if it involves one of the special senses such as sight or smell. In other cases, the psychological distress could be converted into an unusual pattern of motor activity such as a tic or even a seizure (sometimes called a 'pseudoseizure' to differentiate it from seizures that have a physical basis such as epilepsy or a brain tumour). Pseudoseizures can be very difficult to distinguish from organic seizures. One method of telling them apart is to take a blood sample 10–20 minutes after the event and to measure the serum level of the hormone prolactin, which tends to be raised by an organic seizure but unaffected by a pseudoseizure. More invasive but also more reliable is video telemetry, which involves continuous monitoring over several days with both a video camera and an electroencephalograph[14].

Given that all these different types (and there are many more) of somatized symptoms are psychological in origin, are they any less 'real'? It is quite common for the person with somatized symptoms to deny the impact of any traumatic event and even to display a striking lack of concern for his disability (a phenomenon referred to in the psychiatric jargon as *la belle indifférence*), thereby reinforcing any forming impression that the somatized symptoms are not 'genuine'. However, it should be remembered that ego defences are by definition subconscious, and that the somatizing person is therefore not conscious or, at least, not entirely conscious, of the psychological origins of his physical symptoms. To him, the symptoms are entirely real, and they are also entirely real in the important sense that – despite their apparent lack of a biological basis – they do in fact exist, that is, the limb cannot move, the eye cannot see, and so on[15]. For these reasons, some

---

14 An apparatus that records electrical activity along the skull.

15 Similarly, the headaches that I get whenever I end up doing something that I should not be doing (usually involving making money) are very real. Over time, I have learnt to listen to these headaches, and am very much poorer for it.

authorities advocate replacing terms such as 'pseudoseizures' and the even older 'hysterical seizures' with less judgmental terms such as 'psychogenic non-epileptic seizures' that do not inherently imply that the somatized symptoms are in some sense false or fraudulent.

As mentioned in Chapters 7 and 10, it is very common, particularly in traditional societies, for people with what may be construed as depression to present not with psychological complaints but with physical complaints such as fatigue, headache, or chest pain; like many ego defences, this tendency to concretize psychic pain is deeply ingrained in our human nature, and should not be mistaken or misunderstood for a factitious disorder or malingering.

A factitious disorder is defined by physical and psychological symptoms that are manufactured or exaggerated for the purpose of benefitting from the rights associated with the 'sick role'[16], in particular, to attract attention and sympathy, to be exempted from normal social roles, and, at the same time, to be absolved from any blame for the sickness. A factitious disorder with predominantly physical symptoms is sometimes called Münchausen Syndrome, after the 18th century Prussian cavalry officer Baron Münchausen. The Baron was one of the greatest liars in recorded history, and one of the most notorious

---

16   Talcott Parsons, 1951.

of his many 'hair-raising' claims was to have pulled himself out of a swamp by the very hair on his head.

Whereas a factitious disorder is defined by symptoms that are manufactured or exaggerated for the purpose of enjoying the privileges of the sick role, malingering is defined by symptoms that are manufactured or exaggerated for a purpose other than enjoying the privileges of the sick role. This purpose is usually much more concrete and immediate than that of a factitious disorder, for example, claiming compensation, evading the police or criminal justice system, or obtaining a bed for the night. Thus, it is quite clear that somatization has little to do with factitious disorders or malingering; although a person with somatization (as, indeed, most any ill person) may enjoy the privileges of the sick role and may receive material benefits as a result of being ill, neither is his primary purpose.

In recent decades, it has become increasingly clear that psychological stressors can lead to physical symptoms not only by the ego defence of somatization but also by physical processes involving the nervous, endocrine, and immune systems. For example, one recent study conducted by Dr Elizabeth Mostofsky of Harvard Medical School found that the first 24 hours of bereavement are associated with a staggering 21-fold increased risk of a heart attack. Since Robert Ader's initial experiments on lab rats in the 1970s, the field of psychoneuroimmunology has truly blossomed. The large and ever increasing body of evidence that it continues to uncover has led to the mainstream recognition not only of the adverse effects of psychological stress on health, recovery, and ageing, but also of the beneficial effects of positive emotions such as happiness, motivation, and a sense of purpose. Here again, modern science has barely caught up with the wisdom of the Ancients, who were well aware of the strong link between psychological wellbeing and good health.

In one of Plato's early dialogues, the *Charmides*, Socrates tells the young Charmides, who has been suffering from headaches, about a charm for headaches that he has recently learned from one of the mystical physicians to the king of Thrace. According to this physician, however, it is best to cure the soul before curing the body, since health and happiness ultimately depend on the state of the soul. But how should one go about curing the soul? Why, with beautiful words, of course. 'He said the soul was treated with certain charms, my dear Charmides, and that these charms were beautiful words.'

As the virtue of temperance is the marker of the health of the soul, Socrates asks Charmides whether he thinks that he is sufficiently temperate. The *Charmides* takes place in 432 BC, the year of Socrate's return to Athens from military service at the battle of Potidaea, and its subject, as it turns out, is no less than the nature of *sophrosyne*, a philosophical term often translated as 'temperance' but with the etymological meaning of 'healthy mindedness'. As is typical in Plato, the dialogue ends in a state of *aporia* (a state of inconclusive non-knowledge), with Socrates accusing himself of being a worthless inquirer and a 'babbler'. Charmides concludes that he can hardly be expected to know whether he is sufficiently temperate if not even Socrates is able to define temperance for him.

Whereas Plato associates physical and mental health with the virtues and in particular with the virtue of temperance (*sophrosyne*, 'healthy mindedness'), Aristotle associates health with the Supreme Good for man. This Supreme Good, he says, is *eudaimonia*, a philosophical term that is loosely translated as 'happiness', but that is perhaps best translated as 'human flourishing'. In a nutshell, Aristotle argues that to understand the essence of a thing, it is necessary to understand its distinctive function. For example, one cannot understand what it is to be a musician unless one can understand that the distinctive function of a musician is 'to play on a musical instrument with a certain degree of skill'. Whereas human beings need nourishment like plants and have sentience like animals, their distinctive function, says Aristotle, is their unique capacity to reason. Thus, the Supreme Good, or Happiness, for human beings is to lead a life that enables them to exercise and to develop their reason, and that is in accordance with rational principles.

Moreover, to live life according to rational principles is to seek out the right sorts of pleasure, underplaying those brutish, restorative pleasures such as food and sex that are only incidentally pleasurable (by virtue of being restorative), and privileging those higher pleasures such as contemplation and friendship that cannot admit of either pain or excess and that are therefore pleasurable by nature. To pursue the higher pleasures is 'to stimulate the action of the healthy nature'[17], and to be healthy is not only to be free from pain and disease, but also and most importantly to flourish according to our essential nature as human beings. So, although Plato associates health with 'healthy mindedness' and Aristotle with the Supreme Good, once the Supreme Good is unpacked it becomes very clear that this is merely a difference of emphasis, and that Plato and Aristotle are not in any fundamental disagreement on this issue. As Socrates says in the *Lesser Hippias*, 'you will do me a much greater benefit if you were to cure my soul of ignorance, than you would if you were to cure my body of disease.'

---

17 *Nicomachean Ethics*, Book 8.

12. Reaction formation

Displacement, the redirection of uncomfortable feelings towards someone or something less threatening, and somatization, their conversion into more tolerable physical symptoms, are both methods of transforming uncomfortable feelings into some more manageable form. A third method of transforming uncomfortable feelings into a more manageable form is reaction formation, which can be defined as the superficial adoption and, often, exaggeration of ideas and impulses that are diametrically opposed to one's own. For instance a man who finds himself attracted to a person of the same sex may cope with the felt unacceptability of this attraction by over-acting heterosexual: going out for several pints with the lads, speaking in a gruff voice, banging his fists on the counter, whistling at pretty girls, conspicuously engaging in a string of baseless heterosexual relationships, and so on.

A possible high-profile case of reaction formation is that of the Florida Congressman Mark Foley who, as chairman of the Missing and Exploited Children's Caucus, introduced legislation to protect children from exploitation by adults over the Internet. Foley resigned when it later emerged that he had exchanged sexually explicit electronic messages with a teenage boy. Other, classic, examples of reaction formation are the alcoholic who extolls the virtues of abstinence, the rich kid who attends and even organizes anti-capitalist rallies, and the angry person who behaves with exaggerated calm and courtesy.

It should be noted that the angry person who behaves with exaggerated calm and courtesy might nevertheless express his anger through passive-aggressive means, that is, through unconscious resistance to meeting the reasonable expectations of others. Examples of passive-aggressive behaviour include creating doubt and confusion, being late on a regular but unpredictable basis; forgetting or omitting significant items or details; withdrawing usual behaviours such as making a cup of tea, cooking, cleaning, or having sex; and shifting responsibility or blame. As the name suggests, passive-aggressive behaviour is a means of expressing aggression covertly and so without incurring the personal, interpersonal, and social costs of more overt aggression. It does, however, prevent the underlying issues from being identified and resolved, and can lead to a great deal of upset and resentment in the person or people on its receiving end. Relationships with significant elements of passive-aggressive behaviour do not generally last for very long.

An especially interesting instance of reaction formation is that of two people who matter deeply to each other, but who argue all the time to suppress their mutual desire. Typically, A accepts that B is important to him, but B does not accept this of A; thus, B initiates arguments so as to help repress those feelings, and A initiates or participates in arguments so as to help cope with B's rejection, that is, to safeguard his ego, vent his anger, and temper his feelings. Until, that is, he gets bored and leaves.

Another, rather special, instance of reaction formation is the person who hates the group but not the individual members of the group with whom he is personally acquainted. This pattern helps to explain such phenomena as the misogynist who is devoted to his wife or the racist who marries someone from another race. This should be distinguished from something like the converse, which is to think of a hated person as part of a group and then to hate the group instead of the person – an ego defence called generalization. For example, a woman who is upset by her husband's infidelity directs her anger not at him but at the male sex in general. Conversely, a man who has been neglected or abused by his mother is still able to love her but only at the cost of having been turned into an incurable misogynist.

Behaviour that results from reaction formation can be recognized, or as least suspected, as such on the basis that it tends to have something of a manic edge, that is, that it tends to be exaggerated, compulsive, and inflexible. More importantly, perhaps, is that the person's behaviour does not 'add up' in the context of his bigger picture (which he himself may not have in mind), and may appear to the insightful friend or observer as being rather unfounded, irrational, or idiosyncratic. In many cases, the behaviour is also dystonic, that is, out of keeping with the person's ideal self-image, and therefore damaging to his deep-seated goals and ambitions and ultimately to his sense of self-worth. Of course, all this is more or less true not just of reaction formation, but of all forms of self-deception.

If a person is challenged about his self-deceptive behaviour, he usually appears either confused and silent or irritated and evasive. But careful: whereas pointing out a person's ego defences and observing his reaction might lead one to a better understanding of that person, it is bound to cause him significant distress. In terms of helping him, it is likely to be either futile or counterproductive, serving merely to anger or alienate him and to further entrench his ego defences. This is mostly because an ego defence such as reaction formation does not exist in some sort of splendid isolation, but as a symptom or manifestation of some even more profound and pervasive problem – and it is this primary problem, if any at all, that first needs to be carefully addressed, step by step, over a long period of time. The truth cannot blossom unless the forest has first been cleared and the earth painstakingly prepared to receive it. After that, it needs regular pruning, trellising, and irrigation, and it is still several years before it can turn good wine.

Reaction formation may at least partially underlie the apparently paradoxical psychological phenomenon that the criminologist and psychiatrist Nils Bejerot baptized 'Stockholm Syndrome' after the events that took place during the 1973 attempted robbery of the Norrmalmstorg, Stockholm branch of *Kreditbanken*. Jan Erik Olsson, a prisoner on leave, entered the bank with the simple intention of robbing it. When police followed in, he opened fire and injured one policeman. A hostage situation ensued: for six days, from August 23 to August 28, Olsson held four bank employees at gunpoint in the bank's main vault. Olsson demanded, among others, that his friend and old cellmate Clark Olofsson join his operation; once within the bank, Olofsson established a communication link with police negotiators who, despite hearing death threats and screams over the telephone, refused to let the comperes escape with the hostages. Eventually, the police drilled a hole into the vault from the apartment above and launched a gas attack through this hole. Olsson and Olofsson soon surrendered without any of the hostages being seriously injured. But the strange thing is this. After some time in the vault, the hostages began to form an emotional attachment with their captors. They reported fearing the police more than their captors, and, after their release, they refused to testify against Olsson and Olofsson and even set up a fund to cover their legal defence fees. Olofsson claimed that he had not been aiding Olsson but merely trying to contain the situation and safeguard the hostages, and had his convictions quashed by the court of appeal. He became friendly with one of the hostages, Kristin Ehnemark; they met occasionally and even their families became friends.

Another notorious case of Stockholm Syndrome is that of millionaire heiress Patty Hearst (Figure 5), who on February 4, 1974, at the age of 19, was kidnapped from her apartment in Berkeley, California by a left-wing urban guerrilla group calling itself the Symbionese Liberation Army or SLA. On April 3 Hearst announced on an audiotape that she had joined the SLA under the pseudonym of 'Tania', and on April 15 she was photographed wielding an M1 Carbine while robbing a bank in San Francisco. When she was eventually arrested, she listed her occupation as 'urban guerilla' and asked her attorney to 'tell everybody that I'm smiling, that I feel free and strong and I send my greetings and love to all the sisters and brothers out there'. After almost two years in prison, Hirst had her sentence commuted by President Jimmy Carter, and on January 20, 2001, President Bill Clinton granted her a full Presidential Pardon in his last official act before leaving office.

Most of human history has been played out in hunter-gatherer societies in which abductions, particularly of women and their

Figure 5: Jacket of the audio CD of a 2007 radio musical by the Berlin-based duo Stereo Total. The picture of Patty Hearst on the jacket is inspired by a 1974 photograph released for publicity purposes by the Symbionese Liberation Army. In this famous photograph, Hearst is standing in front of the guerrilla group's insignia and wielding a modified full auto M1 Carbine.

dependent children, must have been a frequent occurrence. Thus, it is possible to envisage that the capture-bonding psychological response displayed by Kristin Ehnemark, Patty Hearst, and countless others is not just an ego defence, but also an adaptive trait that promotes survival in times of war and strife. Indeed, an inverse of Stockholm Syndrome called 'Lima Syndrome' has been proposed, in which abductors develop sympathy for their hostages. Lima Syndrome is named after

> Adaptive to survival in relationship

the so-called Japanese Embassy Hostage Crisis: on December 17, 1996 some members of the Túpac Amaru Revolutionary Movement took hostage hundreds of people attending a party to celebrate the birthday of Emperor Akihito at the official residence of the Japanese ambassador to Peru. But within only a few hours the captors had released most of the hostages, including even the most valuable ones. If indeed the capture-bonding response is deeply ingrained in the human psyche, then its activation or partial activation could help to explain not only the counterintuitive behaviour of some hostages, but also that of people who engage and persist in, among others, religious cults, abusive relationships, and sadomasochistic sexual practices.

The ego defence of reaction formation should not be confused with that of undoing, which is the thinking of a thought or carrying out of an act that negates a previous, uncomfortable thought or act. An example of undoing is the absent father who occasionally returns with *grands gestes* to spoil and smother his children. Another example is an angry wife who throws a plate at her husband and then 'makes up for it' by smothering him in kisses. The absent father and angry wife are not merely trying to minimize the consequences of their behaviour, but also, as if by magic, to reverse or erase it in time. A third example of undoing is that of a man who damages a friend's prospects by revealing one of his secrets; then, a few days later, he visits the friend and brings him a small gift. Like reparation (as in the examples above), atonement, repentance, and confession can also represent forms of undoing. A fourth, much less benign, example of undoing is that of a man who is romantically or erotically attracted to another man, and who goes out of his way to insult, assault, or otherwise harm him. Undoing does not necessarily need to involve some kind of contrary or negating action; in some cases, a person might 'undo' a thought or action with the very same thought or action, but this time imputing it with a different and opposite unconscious meaning.

Undoing is commonly seen in obsessive-compulsive disorder or OCD. Common obsessional thoughts in OCD involve doubt (for example that some electrical appliances have not been safely turned off), contamination, orderliness and symmetry, safety, physical symptoms, aggression, and sex. To cope with the anxiety induced by such obsessional thoughts, a person may employ certain acts, which quickly become compulsive, to 'undo' or counteract the obsessional thoughts and obtain temporary relief from the anxiety. For example, a person with an obsession about being contaminated with germs might develop a compulsion to scrub and scour his hands over and over to the point that they bleed. This act can symbolically represent a cleansing out of undesirable thoughts, rather as with Lady Macbeth in Shakespeare's *Macbeth*. 'Here's the smell of the blood still; all the perfumes of Arabia will not sweeten this little hand. Oh, oh, oh!'

13. Minimization

Another method of transforming uncomfortable feelings into something more manageable is to change them in size, for example, to devalue or minimize them. Although the person is conscious of his uncomfortable feelings, he gives them no or little importance and may insist to others that they mean little or nothing to him. Doing the opposite, that is, exaggerating rather than minimizing the impact of uncomfortable feelings, can also achieve a similar purpose. By making a big deal out of a bad situation, the person is able to reassure himself and persuade others that he is normally in control of such situations and therefore perfectly adequate in that particular sphere. Exaggeration can also be used to ignore the true significance of a situation or to defend against anxiety that the situation may persist or deteriorate. For example, a woman who is afraid that her partner might get drunk and cheat on her prevents him from going out with his friends by crying her eyes out and accusing him of neglecting and abandoning her. The mother of an 11-year-old boy who comes back from school with an unusual bad grade scolds and punishes him. Then the next day she gives him a long lecture that concludes with how no one will ever want to employ or marry him. Although there is a part of manipulation in both of these examples, manipulation is not the primary intent and is more subconscious than premeditated.

14. Symbolization

Uncomfortable feelings can also be transformed, or crystal-lized, into a person or object that then acts as a symbol of the uncomfortable feelings. Symbols appear especially in dreams, but can also appear in daydreams or fantasies; in neurotic phenomena such as arachnophobia (fear or spiders), gephydrophobia (fear of crossing bridges), and other phobias; in religious beliefs and practices; in myths and folklore; and in psychotic experiences. Freud himself offers an interpretation of the symbolism of the bridge in his *New Introductory Lessons on Psychoanalysis*.

> *The other symbol I want to talk to you about is that of the bridge, which has been explained by Ferenczi (1921 and 1922). First it means the male organ, which unites the two parents in sexual intercourse; but afterwards it develops further meanings which are derived from this first one. In so far as it is thanks to the male organ that we are able to come into the world at all, out of the*

> *amniotic fluid, a bridge becomes the crossing from*
> *the other world (the unborn state, the womb) to*
> *their world (life); and, since men also picture death*
> *as a return to the womb (to the water), a bridge*
> *also acquires the meaning of something that leads*
> *to death, and finally, at a further remove from its*
> *original sense, it stands for transitions or changes*
> *in condition generally...*

Several repressed thoughts and feelings can be amalgamated or condensed into a single symbol, such that many of the products of symbolization are in fact, so to speak, composite symbols. This enables dreams to be more compact and coherent than the repressed thoughts that they in part represent.

Parapraxes or Freudian slips provide some insight into the ego defence of condensation. Parapraxes are basically 'faulty actions' that occur when unconscious thoughts and desires suddenly parallel and then override conscious thoughts and intentions, for instance, calling a partner by the name of an ex-partner, substituting one word for another that rhymes or sounds similar ('I would like to thank/spank you', 'You are a vast repository/suppository of information'), or combining two words into a single word ('Let us withdraw to the dining room for supfer (supper/suffer)', 'He is a very lustrous man (illustrious/lustful)'). Parapraxes often manifest in speech, but might also manifest in writing, physical actions, and memories, and even in mishearings, misreadings, and the mislaying of objects. Freud held that parapraxes are one of only four direct routes into the unconscious, the other three being jokes, free association, and dreams, which he famously called 'the royal road to the unconsious'. To shed some more light on the processes of symbolization and condensation, I shall first relate and then interpret one of my most recent dreams.

I slept in late last Wednesday and awoke naturally from a rather interesting dream, which I quickly jotted down into my notebook. A great problem of modern living is the waking up to an alarm clock, which interrupts sleep before dreams can be completed. This denies the opportunity to test and explore thoughts and feelings, and so to attain the sort of insight and understanding that might put an end to waking up to an alarm clock. This is just one of the many meanings of 'being trapped by the 9 to 5'. Moving on to my dream, I was about 17 years old, and not much different from my current, adult self. I was perhaps in my final year at secondary school, in the rural hills overlooking Lake Geneva. On a clear day, it might have been possible to make out the snow-capped Alps beyond the lake, but on that late morning the sky was clouded over. It must also have been early spring, since the seed that had been sown into the bare but loamy fields had only just begun to sprout. I felt harried and out of control, assailed by timetables, assignments, deadlines, social pressures, and thoughts about my future, and so I made an appointment with the school counsellor[18]. I sat on a chair in her room, which was in an old farmhouse on the school grounds, and began telling her about my predicament. She, however, was not interested. She was lying on a couch covered by a blanket, and every so often would lift the blanket to reveal her bare breasts. After some time, a friend or colleague of hers arrived; she stepped out to greet him and through the window I could see them chatting away. I felt quite angry with the counsellor and, to pass the time, I began to explore her room and in particular her bookcase. Therein I picked up a dusty leather-bound volume, *The World as Will*, by Arthur Schopenhauer. Holding the book in my hands, I was struck with such wonder and amazement that I began to weep. Without waiting for the counsellor to return, I stepped out of the room and onto High Holborn, London, at which point I awoke.

What do I make of this dream? In the dream, I was young and of an age to learn. The sky was clouded over, mirroring my then feelings. The seed in the rich, fertile earth had begun to sprout, auguring my own growth and rebirth. I sought help from the person best qualified to help me, but, like so many people, she turned out to be immature, self-motivated, and of no help at all. She was lying on the couch while I was sitting in a chair, perhaps indicating that she needed therapy more

---

18 The school counselor is not based on any real person, and is entirely a product of my symbolization and condensation.

than I did, or that I understood or would come to understand more than she did. The book represented my salvation, which was not to come through the counsellor and by extension through school and society, but through the thoughts of the greatest minds and by extension through philosophy. The title of the book, *The World as Will*, was particularly significant because it connoted freedom of the will, which is the cure for helplessness and the particular gift of philosophy as broadly conceived. My weeping represented a cathartic ('cleansing') release brought about by sudden insight, which, as mentioned in Chapter 2, is an important goal of classical psychoanalytic psychotherapy. Upon stepping out of the room, I was no longer trapped on school premises but liberated into the wider world as symbolized by Holborn ('whole-born').

In his *General Aspects of Dream Psychology*, the pre-eminent psychiatrist and psychotherapist Carl Jung argues that dreams contribute to the self-regulation of the psyche by automatically bringing up everything that is repressed or neglected or unknown. However, he continues, their compensatory significance is often not immediately apparent because of our still very incomplete knowledge of the nature and the needs of the human psyche. Yet, some 2,000 years before the time of Jung and Freud, thinkers such as Plato, Aristotle, and the 1st century Hellenistic philosopher Philo of Alexandria already held some fairly advanced notions in the still uncreated field of dream psychology. For instance, in the *Politicus*, Plato says that 'every man seems to know all things in a dreamy sort of way, and then again to wake up and know nothing'. Aristotle wrote a book entitled *On Divination in Sleep*, in which he argues that skilful dream interpretation calls upon the faculty of observing resemblances. He then compares dream presentations to the forms reflected in water: if the motion in the water is great, then the reflection bears little resemblance to its original, and particular skill is required on the part of the dream interpreter. In his treatise *On Sleep*, Philo of Alexandria offers four different interpretations for the ladder to heaven that appears in Jacob's dream (Figure 6). This dream is retold in the Book of Genesis, which antedates Plato and Aristotle by several centuries.

> *And Jacob went out from Beersheba, and went toward Haran. And he lighted upon a certain place, and tarried there all night, because the sun was set; and he took of the stones of that place, and put them for his pillows, and lay down in that place to sleep. And he dreamed, and behold a ladder set up on the earth, and the top of it reached to heaven: and behold the angels of God ascending and descending on it. And, behold, the LORD stood above it, and said, I am the LORD God of Abraham thy father, and the God of Isaac: the land whereon thou liest, to thee will I give it, and to thy seed; And thy seed shall be as the dust*

*of the earth, and thou shalt spread abroad to the
west, and to the east, and to the north, and to the
south: and in thee and in thy seed shall all the
families of the earth be blessed. And, behold, I am
with thee, and will keep thee in all places whither
thou goest, and will bring thee again into this
land; for I will not leave thee, until I have done
that which I have spoken to thee of. And Jacob
awakened out of his sleep, and he said, Surely the
LORD is in this place; and I knew it not.*

I am not particularly keen on any of Philo's four interpretations
and much prefer the 4th century interpretation of St Gregory
the Theologian and St John Chrysostom, who thought of the
ladder in terms of an ascetic path of virtue along which it is
possible for man to ascend from earth to heaven, 'not using
material steps, but improvement and correction of manners'.
The notion of dream interpretation far antedates the birth of
psychoanalysis, and probably served an important function in
most, if not all, historical societies. In having lost this function,
modern man has also lost the best part of his nature, which
he obliviously passes on to the next generation of dreamers.

As I said, symbols appear not only in dreams, daydreams,
and fantasies, but also in myths and folklore and in psychotic
experiences, among others. For example, Carl Jung suggested
that the hero's slaying of the dragon is a projection of the

Figure 6: An angel descends Jacob's ladder on the west front of Bath Abbey. Bath stone. Photograph by Brian Robert Marshall.

struggle of the adolescent ego for deliverance from parental dominance. Jung himself experienced 'a confrontation with the unconscious', most likely a psychotic episode, in which, like the mythological hero, he travelled deep down into an abyssal underworld to confront and conquer his daemons.

There he conversed with Salome, a beautiful woman whom he thought of as the archetype of the feminine, and Philemon, an old man with a white beard and the wings of a kingfisher, the archetype of the wise old man. Far more than mere one-time apparitions, Salome and Philemon took on lives of their own and said things that Jung had not previously thought. In Philemon, Jung felt that he had at long last found the father figure that he had forever been searching for, and that both Freud and his own father, the pitiable pastor Paul Jung, had singularly failed to be. More than a father figure, Philemon was a guru, and the prefigurement of that which Jung himself was later to become: the 'wise old man of Zürich'. After re-emerging into sanity at the end of the First World War, Jung considered that he had found in his madness 'the *prima materia* for a lifetime's work'.

15. Reification

There has never been a time when you and I have
not existed, nor will there be a time when we will
cease to exist.

   – Bhagavad Gita

The ego defence of reification involves turning an abstract
and difficult problem into something much more concrete and
comprehensible. Reification has already been touched upon in
the context of depression (Chapter 9): by thinking of human
distress in terms of a biological illness such as depression, a
person is able to avoid facing up to the important psychological
or life problems that are at the root of his suffering. Another
example of reification is the common, almost cartoonish
conception of God as a man in a long robe and large beard.
Man first creates the universe in his image, and then turns
round to say that God created man is His image: 'So God
created man in his own image, in the image of God created

he him; male and female created he them.[19]' As Voltaire quipped, if God created man in his image, man has returned the compliment.

The 5th and 6th century BC philosopher Xenophanes of Colophon, who roamed throughout the Mediterranean for 67 years and lived for about 100, rails against the poets Hesiod and Homer (and the large majority of his contemporaries) for anthropomorphizing the gods. He says,

> *Yes, and if oxen and horses or lions had hands, and could paint with their hands, and produce works of art as men do, horses would paint the forms of the gods like horses, and oxen like oxen, and make their bodies in the image of their several kinds... The Ethiopians make their gods black and snub-nosed; the Thracians say theirs have blue eyes and red hair.*

Instead, Xenophanes suggests that there is a single god that is 'greatest among gods and men' and 'not at all mortal in body or thought'. As he assimilates this god with the cosmos and thinks of it as abstract and unchanging, he is sometimes regarded as an early monotheist. Xenophanes also recognizes that if knowledge can only ever be attained through sense

---

19 Genesis 1:27.

experience, then knowledge of the underlying nature of reality is unattainable. For even if sense experience is objective, which it is not[20], the underlying nature of reality is not amenable to observation by sense experience. Thus, the best that can be hoped for is not knowledge, but true belief. Plato also makes this distinction, notably in the *Meno* in which Socrates compares true beliefs to the moving statues of Daedalus[21] which cannot be fixed to the ground unless 'fastened by the tie of the cause', whereupon they cease being true beliefs and become knowledge. For all this, man is embodied and trusting to his senses; he had sooner believe in a sensible improbability than in an insensible uncertainty, that is, sooner worship an idol than grapple with the philosophers.

The very purpose of an ego defence such as reification (or indeed any ego defence) is, as the name implies, to protect and uphold a certain crystallized notion of the self or 'I'. There is therefore an important sense in which the reifying self is itself reified. To understand this better, it is helpful to enquire into the nature of the self. The question of the nature of the self is one that I discuss at some length in *The Art of Failure,* and I have included here only the main lines of my argument.

---

20 For example, the sense experience of a insect, fish, or bat is completely different to ours.

21 A mythological architect and craftsman of unsurpassed skill.

According to the 17th century philosopher John Locke, a person is a person because he can think about himself in the past, future, and conditional, and in a variety of different places. In other words, a person is a person because he has a permanent self that can persist through the vagaries of space and time. This being so, one might expect to be able to locate the seat of this permanent self, and by far the most likely candidates are the body and the brain.

It is almost immediately possible to rule out the body on the grounds that, if a person is left completely and permanently brain-dead, then he is no longer considered to be a person even though his body is still alive, that is, even though his organs are still being perfused with oxygenated blood. Indeed, it is on these very grounds that his relatives might give permission for his organs to be donated. If this seems unconvincing, let us imagine together with the contemporary philosopher Sydney Shoemaker that science has advanced to the point that brain transplants are possible. Two men, Brown and Robinson, each have their brains removed and operated on at the same time, but a poorly trained assistant inadvertently puts Brown's brain into Robinson's head and *vice versa*. One of these entities dies, but the one with Brown's brain and Robinson's body – let us call him Brownson – survives. Most people would argue that Brownson is in fact Brown, just as a person who undergoes a face transplant or a sex change very much remains the same person after the operation. Does this mean that the permanent self must be located in the brain?

Brownson is Brown either because he has Brown's brain or because he is psychologically continuous with Brown, that is, because his mental states derive or descend from those of Brown. To help clear up this particular problem, let us imagine that Brownson's brain has been neatly bisected and that each hemisphere, the right and the left, is transplanted into a brainless body of its own. After the operation, two people awake who are both psychologically continuous with Brownson. Are both these people Brownson? And if so, are they also each other? Most people would agree that, upon awaking, the pair are very similar to each other, but that with the passage of time they will develop and diverge into noticeably different people, much as in the case of identical twins one of whom may become an unmarried accountant and the other a married concert pianist with three children. Thus, although selfhood depends causally upon the existence of the brain, it amounts to something far more than just the brain. This something is vague and intangible, and might best be described, I think, as a semi-fictional narrative that is in constant need of writing and editing.

It is quite natural to think of the self as something concrete, but it is, in fact, nothing of the sort. Rather, it is an abstract product of our minds, a convenient concept or schema that enables us to relate our present self with our past, future, and conditional selves, and thereby to create an illusion of coherence and continuity from a big jumble of disparate experiences. Indeed, one could go so far as to argue that the self is nothing but the sum total of our ego defences, and that it is therefore tantamount to one gigantic ego defence, namely, the ego itself. The self is like a cracked mask that is in constant need of being pieced together (Figure 7). But behind the mask there is nobody at home.

Figure 7: Marcus Aurelius, philosopher and Roman emperor. Fragment of a bronze portrait. 'Very little is needed to make a happy life; it is all within yourself, in your way of thinking.'

A number of Eastern philosophies also hold that the ego is something of an illusion. Buddhism, for instance, teaches the concept of the 'not-self' (*anattā*), which is composed of the five elements (*skandhas*) of body, sensation, perception, will, and consciousness. These five elements are in a constant state of change but together create the illusion of continuity, that is, the illusion of the self. For this reason, a person cannot, even with the greatest effort of concentration, ever become conscious of any core self, but only and at most of such and such fleeting perception, thought, or feeling. This ancient Eastern account of the self could have been written off as mystical had it not also been shared by such giants of the canon as the 18th century empirical philosopher David Hume. Thus, in his *Treatise of Human Nature*, Hume says:

> *When I enter most intimately into what I call myself, I always stumble on some particular perception or other, of heat or cold, light or shade, love or hatred, pain or pleasure. I can never catch myself at any time without a perception, and never can observe anything but the perception. When my perceptions are removed for any time, as by sound sleep, so long am I insensible of myself, and may truly be said not to exist.*

Our ego defences as broadly conceived – that is, not only our ego defences proper but also our moral codes, bourgeois values, habits, customs, culture, and other ties – may provide us with an illusion of the self, but they also define us as such and such and, in so doing, constrain our range of thought, feeling, and action and thereby our freedom not only to do what we want but also, and more fundamentally, to want what we want. Thus, the elements that provide us with the illusion of the self are, paradoxically, the very same elements that prevent us from fulfilling our true potential as human beings.

According to the Buddha, the failure to recognize the illusion of the self is the source of all ignorance and unhappiness. It is only by renouncing the self, that is, by dropping his ego defences and committing metaphorical suicide, that a person can open up to different modes of being and relating and thereby transform himself into a pure essence of humanity. In so doing, he becomes free to recast himself as a much more joyful and productive person, and attains the only species of transcendence and immortality that is open to man.

PART IIIA: EVASION THROUGH FRAUD OR FANTASY

In contrast to abstraction, which involves ignoring or suppressing the source of the anxiety so that it no longer seems to exist, and transformation, which involves converting the anxiety into some more manageable form, evasion involves distracting oneself from the anxiety so as to minimize its threat and impact. This can be achieved through (1) fraud, (2) fantasy, (3) one's relation with other people, or (4) one's relation with the world. Part IIIA treats of fraud and fantasy, Part IIIB of people and the world.

16. Vagueness

A person may be vague and tangential in discussing certain uncomfortable feelings, events, or situations, or may disclose the source of the discomfort but then fail to elaborate upon its details or emotional implications. It is not so much that he wishes to hide these matters from other people, but more that he does not wish to bring them into the limelight of his conscious attention where they will be at their most glaring and painful. In this respect, vagueness is on the same spectrum as repression, only not so marked. It is often evident after an episode of self-harm or attempted suicide, in which case it may appear exaggerated by the personal nature of the subject matter, the fear of stigma or recrimination, and the felt distance of the mental healthcare professionals involved.

Even more elaborate than vagueness is frankness, which superficially appears to be the opposite of vagueness. The person puts on the guise of being forthright and forthcoming but does not reveal the whole truth, picking and choosing those aspects of the truth – and especially those aspects of the truth concerning other people – that best serve his purposes. As with vagueness, frankness may be a means of holding back uncomfortable material from the forefront of conscious attention. However, if there are hostile overtones or if the frankness forms part of a wider pattern of aggressive or antisocial behaviour, then it is more likely to represent a defence against poor self-esteem or the fear of victimization.

Another, related, unconscious stratagem for holding back material from the forefront of conscious attention is to privilege one emotion over one or several others so that it comes to monopolize centre stage at the expense of the other, more uncomfortable, emotions. Examples of this ego defence, which is called 'one affect versus another', include the jilted lover who feels angry rather than saddened and hurt (anger being in this case the less painful emotion); the parents of a child who has committed a violent offense who focus on love and forgiveness rather than on anger, disappointment, and shame; and a bisexual person who selectively nurtures his heterosexual impulses and interests so as to crowd out his homosexual ones.

17. Inauthenticity

The three subterfuges described in the preceding chapter – vagueness, frankness, and the privileging of one emotion over another – essentially have to do with the focus of conscious attention. On an altogether different plane is the ego defence of inauthenticity. Inauthenticity involves pretending to be other than one really is, and thereby to cast off the freedom to develop, express, and fulfil one's true self. Inauthenticity is often reinforced by sociocultural forces such as parental expectations, peer pressure, and advertising, and is motivated by the subconscious desires to fit in, avoid criticism, and – in particular – minimize or put off the existential anxiety associated with choice and responsibility. Examples include the teenager who acts 'cool', the person who takes an interest in something because others do, and the person who gets married because he has arrived at the ripe old age of 30, 35, or 40 years old.

The 20th century philosopher Jean-Paul Sartre calls such inauthenticity *mauvaise foie* or 'bad faith'. His paradigmatic example of bad faith is that of a waiter who does his utmost to conform to the archetype of the waiter, that is, to everything that a waiter should or is expected to be. For Sartre, the waiter's exaggerated behaviour is evidence enough that he is play-acting at being a waiter, an automaton whose essence is to be a waiter. By sticking with the safe, easy, default 'choice' and failing to entertain or even recognise the multitude of other choices that are open to him, the waiter places himself at the mercy of his external circumstances. In this important respect, he is more akin to an object – a 'waiter' – than to a conscious human being who is able to transcend his existence to give shape to his essence. As Freud commented in his book, *Civilization and its Discontents*, 'Most people do not really want freedom, because freedom involves responsibility, and most people are frightened of responsibility.'

The concept of authenticity does not begin with Sartre or Freud, and stretches at least as far back as Plato. In the *Greater Alcibiades*, Socrates asks a young and foolish Alcibiades how one is to go about gaining self-knowledge. Socrates maintains that, if one were to say to the eye, 'See yourself,' the eye should look into a mirror to see itself. Since the pupil of the eye is just like a mirror, the eye could see itself by looking into an eye. Similarly, the soul can see itself by looking into the soul, and particularly into that part of the soul which has most to do with wisdom and which is therefore most akin to the divine. Self-knowledge, Socrates concludes, is, in fact, no other than wisdom; unless Alcibiades finds wisdom, he will never be able to know his own good and evil, nor that of others, nor the affairs of states. If Alcibiades were to become a statesman – as indeed he intends – without first having found wisdom, he would fall into error and be miserable, and make everybody else miserable too. What is more, he who is not wise cannot be happy, and it is better for such a person to be commanded by a superior in wisdom; since that which is better is also more becoming, slavery is more becoming to such a person. Socrates' conclusions may seem abhorrent to modern sensitivities, but it does stand to reason that the person who unconsciously defines himself according to the likes and expectations of others and, by extension, of the society in which he happens to have been born, also condemns himself to by far the most dishonourable kind of slavery: the slavery of the mind.

> *I wander thro' each charter'd street,*
> *Near where the charter'd Thames does flow.*
> *And mark in every face I meet,*
> *Marks of weakness, marks of woe.*
>
> *In every cry of every Man,*
> *In every Infant's cry of fear,*
> *In every voice, in every ban,*
> *The mind-forg'd manacles I hear.*
> ...

William Blake, *London*

As noted by the 20th century psychoanalyst and philosopher Erich Fromm, the authentic person does not necessarily need to resemble some kind of freak outsider. If a person engages in a frank and thorough appraisal of the universal and personal implications of the prevailing social norms and then decides to adopt some or most of them *en toute connaissance de cause*, then he cannot be taxed with inauthenticity. Conversely, it should not be assumed that every eccentric is an authentic. Genuine authenticity lies not so much in the madness as in the method.

A phenomenon that is related to inauthenticity is 'groupthink', a term that is associated with social psychologist Irving Janis. Groupthink is the likely psychological explanation for the maxim that a camel is a horse designed by a committee. It occurs when the members of a group unconsciously seek to minimize conflict by failing to critically test, analyse, and evaluate ideas. As a result, the decisions reached by the group tend to be more irrational than those that would have been reached by any one member of the group acting alone. Groupthink occurs because members of a group are afraid of being criticized and of upsetting the group by criticizing others, and also because of the hubristic feelings of confidence and invulnerability that comes from being in a group. Examples of groupthink disasters studied by Janis include the failure to anticipate the attack on Pearl Harbour, the Bay of Pigs, and the escalation of the Vietnam War. Even dyads such as married couples can fall into groupthink, for example, when they decide to take their holidays in places that neither wanted, but simply thought that the other wanted. This corresponds to a particular form of groupthink called the Abilene Paradox, in which a group decides on a course of action that actually runs counter to the wishes of every individual in the group.

18. Reconstruction of reality

Whereas inauthenticity has to do with the self, reconstruction of reality has more to do with the self's relation to the world; thus, whereas inauthenticity involves pretending to be other than one really is, reconstruction of reality involves pretending that a situation is other than it really is. For example, a teenager has a hard talk with her boyfriend following which she tells him that she is breaking off their relationship. They remain friends, and after some weeks, her ex-boyfriend asks, 'Remember when I dumped you?' In a bid to protect his ego and avoid a futile argument, she bites her lip and lets its pass. One sunny afternoon, a young man decides to go out rowing on a river and, as an afterthought, invites his otherwise unoccupied housemate to join him in the boat. Several months later, his housemate falls in love with him. When he persists in rejecting her advances, she accuses him of having 'led her on'. When he asks in what way, she brings up that sunny afternoon and paints the boat trip as a romantic date. There had been, she insists, 'electricity in the air'.

19. Confabulation

Inauthenticity and reconstruction of reality both present a distorted reality, whether of the self or of the self's relation to the world; in contrast, confabulation puts forth a made-up alternative reality that may be more or less fantastical. Confabulation differs from lying, first, in that the person lacks insight into the falsity of his claims, and, second, in that his intention is to deceive himself rather than others. Confabulation is relatively rare in healthy people, but is common in certain organic amnestic states such as Alzheimer's disease and Wernicke-Korsakoff syndrome and in certain psychological reactions such as dissociative amnesia and fugue (Chapter 4).

Wernicke encephalopathy is a medical emergency precipitated by thiamine (i.e. vitamin B1) deficiency, most commonly secondary to alcohol dependence in developed countries and to starvation in developing countries. Treatment involves intravenous or intramuscular thiamine, but only 20% of sufferers recover, and 10% die from haemorrhages in the brainstem and hypothalamus. The remainder go on to develop Korsakoff syndrome, an irreversible amnestic condition in which confabulation is often a prominent feature.

According to one recent study, confabulation in Korsakoff syndrome tends to be provoked by open questions rather than closed (yes/no) questions, and by questions pertaining to episodic memory, that is, memory for autobiographical events and experiences, rather than questions pertaining to semantic memory, that is, memory for general facts and concepts such as the capital of France and the rules of football. From personal experience, this pattern of confabulation is seen not only in Korsakoff confabulation but also in most other cases of confabulation, and is the general pattern in confabulation. It appears likely, therefore, that in most if not all cases, confabulation represents an unconscious attempt to fill in autobiographical gaps and thereby to maintain a continuous and coherent sense of self.

Given that such confabulated material has no factual basis and has to be created *ex nihilo*, there is no reason for it not to be in rather than out of keeping with the person's ideal self-image; in other words, there is no reason for it not to be egosyntonic rather than egodystonic. This in itself is likely to account for the often idealized or fantastical nature of confabulated material, which may be so implausible as to be difficult to distinguish from a psychotic episode with prominent delusions and hallucinations. For example, an 85-year-old woman with advanced Alzheimer's disease maintains that she is in a hotel in Marbella rather than in a southern English nursing home. She says that she is making plans for her wedding, and is mildly annoyed at the staff, including at myself, for getting in the way of those plans. Upon being asked what she did yesterday, she replies, with a twinkle in her eye, that she hit the town for her hen night, and that her good and glamorous friends spoilt her rotten with champagne and fancy cocktails. Is this confabulation or an elaborate systematized delusion? Or perhaps just a frantic attempt to escape from a despicable reality?

20. Splitting

Instead of changing the focus of attention as in vagueness, frankness, and one affect versus another, distorting reality as in inauthenticity and reconstruction of reality, or making up an alternative reality as in confabulation, the person moves instead or in addition to simplify and schematize reality through, in particular, the ego defences of splitting and deanimation.

Splitting is a very common ego defence that can be defined as the division or polarization of beliefs, actions, objects, or people into good and bad by selectively focusing on either their positive or negative attributes. This is often seen in politics, for example, when members of the Labour Party portray members of the Conservative Party as narrow-minded and self-interested, and, conversely, when members of the Conservative Party caricature members of the Labour Party as self-righteous hypocrites. Other examples of splitting are the religious zealot who pigeonholes people into blessed or damned, the child of divorced parents who idolizes one parent but shuns the other, and the hospital in-patient who sees the doctors as helpful and dedicated but the nurses as lazy and incompetent.

An example of splitting from literature can be found in JD Salinger's *Catcher in the Rye*. The main protagonist, Holden Caulfield, is mystified by adulthood. To help cope with his fear of becoming an adult, he thinks of adulthood as a world of entirely bad things such as superficiality and hypocrisy ('phoniness') and of childhood as a world of entirely good things such as innocence, curiosity, and honesty. He tells his younger sister Phoebe that he imagines childhood as an idyllic field of rye in which children romp and play, and himself as the 'catcher in the rye' who stands on the edge of a cliff, catching the children as they threaten to fall over (and presumably die/ become adults).

> *Anyway, I keep picturing all these little kids playing some game in this big field of rye and all. Thousands of little kids, and nobody's around – nobody big, I mean – except me. And I'm standing on the edge of some crazy cliff. What I have to do, I have to catch everybody if they start to go over the cliff – I mean if they're running and they don't look where they're going I have to come out from somewhere and catch them. That's all I'd do all day. I'd just be the catcher in the rye and all. I know it's crazy, but that's the only thing I'd really like to be.*

In contrast to JD Salinger, Miguel de Cervantes uses splitting to great comical effect in his novel *Don Quixote*. In this novel, the self-appointed and self-styled knight-errant Don Quixote de la Mancha (Figure 8) guides the reader through a mediaeval landscape that he has repopulated with heroes and villains, princesses and harlots, giants and dwarves – with the heroes being the greatest, the villains the most cruel, the ladies the fairest and most virtuous, and so on. 'Take care, your worship,' cries Sancho Pancha, the unfortunate peasant that Don Quixote elevated into his squire, 'those things over there are not giants but windmills.'

Splitting diffuses the anxiety that arises from our inability to grasp the nuances and complexities of a given situation or state of affairs by simplifying and schematizing it, and so making it easier to think about; in addition, it reinforces our sense of self as good and virtuous by effectively demonizing all those who do not share in our opinions and values. On the other hand, such a compartmentalization of opposites leaves us with a distinctly distorted picture of reality and a restricted range of thoughts and emotions; it also affects our ability to attract and maintain relationships, not only because it is tedious and unbecoming, but also because it can easily flip, with friends and lovers being thought of as personified virtue at one time and then as personified vice at another.

Figure 8: Don Quixote de la Mancha with Sancho Panza, by Gustave Doré. Wood engraving. 'The trouble is, Sancho… you are so afraid that you cannot see or hear properly; for one of the effects of fear is to disturb the senses and cause things to appear other than what they are.'

Splitting (together with projection and projective identification, among others) is commonly employed in borderline
personality disorder (BPD), so called because it was thought
to lie on the 'borderline' between neurotic (anxiety) disorders
such as phobias and panic disorder and psychotic disorders
such as schizophrenia and bipolar affective disorder. The
person with BPD essentially lacks a sense of self as a result
of which he experiences feelings of emptiness and fears of
abandonment. There is a pattern of intense but unstable
relationships, emotional instability, outbursts of anger and
violence (especially in response to criticism), and impulsive
and potentially destructive behaviour. Suicidal threats and
acts of self-harm are common, for which reason people with
BPD often come to medical and, in particular, psychiatric
attention.

Splitting also arises in groups, when members of the in-group
are seen to have mostly positive attributes, whereas members
of out-groups are seen to have mostly negative attributes
– a phenomenon that contributes to groupthink (Chapter
17). Finally, it is worth noting that both fairy tales and
Christianity feature a number of sharp splits, for example,
heroes and villains, good and evil, heaven and hell, angels and
demons, and saints and sinners, and that some of the greatest
characters in literature, such as the Achilles or the Odysseus
of Homer and the Anthony or the Cleopatra of Shakespeare,
contain large measures of both good and bad, with the one

being intimately related to the other. As Domitius Enobarbus says of Cleopatra,

> *Age cannot wither her, nor custom stale*
> *Her infinite variety: other women cloy*
> *The appetites they feed: but she makes hungry*
> *Where most she satisfies; for vilest things*
> *Become themselves in her: that the holy priests*
> *Bless her when she is riggish.*

21. Deanimation

The ego defence of deanimation (or dehumanization) involves seeing other people as less or other than human so as not to have to think about them so much and/or feel guilty for neglecting or abusing them. One example of deanimation is that of a person who thinks of his partner or child as a pet or even a great teddy bear so as to better forgive his many failings. Deanimation is easier if the target people are marked out as being different, perhaps by age, gender, race, religion, social class, disability, sexual orientation, or even so little as a different style of dress. Thus, in everyday life, it is all too common to see people in uniform such as waiters, cleaners, bus drivers, and police officers being treated as mere automatons completely devoid of human attributes like feelings or families.

In April 2011, riots broke out in Bristol, England over the opening of a new supermarket. During the riots, Benjamin Cyster dropped a five stone concrete block from the top of a building onto an advancing line of police officers. The block caught PC Nicholas Fry square on the shoulder, knocking him flat to the ground. Instead of expressing anguish or remorse, Cyster continued rioting, and even exclaimed, 'I want to find that copper I hit on the head. I want to do it again.' During Cyster's trial (he received a total sentence of 11-and-a-half years), the court heard that Fry was recovering, but could not bring himself to tell his wife and three children about what Cyster had done to him for fear of upsetting them.

Diane Davies, a 62-year-old grandmother of nine from Anglesey in Wales, was holidaying in one of the most exclusive areas of Barbados. Then one day, in broad daylight, she was brutally raped by a complete stranger. One year on, in November 2011, she decided to talk about her ordeal in a national newspaper so as to expose the shabby treatment that she received from the island's authorities. Of particular note is that she felt certain that she would have been killed had she not remembered reading that a victim of attempted rape should talk to the rapist so that he might see her as a person rather than as an object of gratification. 'So I told him I was a 61-year-old grandmother with four children and nine grandchildren and felt he slightly softened. I think talking to him saved my life.'

Unfortunately, deanimation is not limited to thugs and rapists, and may also be employed by supposedly decent, middle class people. For example, it is commonly employed by healthcare professionals to cope with distress at loss, grief, disease, and death – with patients being referred to by their diagnosis rather than by their name ('the stroke in bed number 6', 'the fractured hip in A&E'...), or just being thought of in terms of a long line of faceless 'patients'. In the early 1970s, the psychologist Philip Zimbardo and his colleagues set up a mock prison with hidden cameras and microphones in the basement of Stanford University's psychology building. The researchers selected 24 healthy, well adjusted undergraduate students, mostly white and middle class men, and randomly assigned them to the roles of either prisoner or guard. The 'prisoners' were to remain in the mock prison 24-hours a day, while the 'guards' were to 'work' in three-man teams over eight-hour shifts. The experiment – which, not surprisingly, has been heavily criticized for its ethics – had been set to run for 14 days, but had to be stopped after just six days due to the aggressive and abusive behaviour of the 'guards' and the extreme adverse psychological reactions of the 'prisoners', five of whom had had to be released early. Even Zimbardo, who had been acting as the prison warden, had overlooked the dehumanizing behaviour of the guards until graduate student Christina Maslach voiced objections to him. In his subsequent book, *The Lucifer Effect,* Zimbardo candidly looks back over the experiment and says, 'Only a few people were able to resist the situational temptations to yield to power and dominance while maintaining some semblance of morality and decency; obviously I was not among that noble class.' The Stanford Prison Experiment attracted a lot of interest after the horrific abuses that took place in the Abu Ghraib prison in

Iraq, and is often upheld to demonstrate the important effect that situation can have on human behaviour.

Deanimation is particularly common during times of war, when it may be incited by governments in a bid to prosecute, or quell opposition to, the war. If people can be seen as less than human, then they become dispensable, and any atrocity can be justified. Thus, Josef Goebbels, the Minister of 'Public Enlightenment and Propaganda' in Hitler's Nazi regime, ruthlessly employed all contemporary methods of propaganda to inflame already existing anti-Semitic feelings. By pinning the blame for all the economic and social ills of the time on the Jewish people and then lampooning them as an 'inferior race', Goebbels prepared the ground for the progressive elimination of their rights and freedoms and, one thing leading to the next, for the mass genocide of the Holocaust.

22. Daydreaming

Whereas evasion through fraud entails conceiving of things as other than they really are, evasion through fantasy entails finding escape in our thoughts. For example, the ego defence of rumination involves holding repetitive and pointless internal debates, often about pseudo-philosophical issues. Rumination should not be confused with intellectualization (Chapter 5), which involves thinking about a problem in cold, abstract, clinical, scientific, or technical terms. Apart from anything else, intellectualization has a completely different feel to rumination, with the person appearing not perplexed but stimulated by the problem in hand.

Another ego defence that entails evasion through fantasy is daydreaming. To daydream is to create an image in the mind's waking eye. This image should be distinguished from an illusion, which is a sense percept that arises as a misinterpretation of a stimulus, for example, hearing voices in rustling leaves, and also from a hallucination, which is a sense percept that arises in the absence of a stimulus, for example, hearing voices despite there being no one about. In contrast to a hallucination, a daydream is experienced as arising from the mind (inner space) rather than from the sense organs (outer space); also, it is not as vivid or lifelike as a true perception and neither is it mistaken for one. The purposes of a daydream are manifold: perhaps to escape from a dull or painful reality; to test, play out, or fulfil a fantasy; to put off the need to act boldly and decisively; to relax and recuperate; and perhaps even to find creative inspiration.

Daydreaming should be distinguished from a fixation on an idealized but improbable future, an ego defence called 'displacement to the future'. Living with some kind of fairy tale ending in mind enables a person not only to distract himself from a less than ideal present but also to absolve himself from coming to terms with reality and taking charge of his destiny. Walt Disney's productions have been criticized on very similar grounds: by editing out some of the harsh realities featured in the original stories, Disney not only presents a misleading account of life's great challenges, but also diminishes the ability of the hero or heroine – and, by extension, the younger and more impressionable members of the audience – to triumph over greater adversity.

And yet the Disney formula could not be more popular. Disney's first full-length animated feature, *Snow White and the Seven Dwarves*, premiered on December 21, 1937 at the

Carthay Circle Theatre in Los Angeles, with the curtain falling on a standing ovation. *Snow White* became the most successful motion picture of 1938, earning over $8 million on its initial release. With the Great Depression in full swing, millions of people readily parted with bare necessities to pay for 83 minutes of pure, undiluted fantasy.

23. Regression

A person can escape into the past just as he can escape into the future, either focusing on an idealized past as he might on an idealized future, or regressing to a state of earlier development or lesser consciousness. Perhaps the most extreme form of regression in the face of emotionally disturbing material is to – quite literally – fall out of consciousness, that is, to faint or fall asleep.

For Freud, human behaviour is primarily motivated by the sex drive or 'libido' (*Latin*, I desire). Even in children the libido is the primary motivating force, and children must progress through various stages of psychosexual development before they can reach psychosexual maturity. Each one of these stages of psychosexual development (except for the fourth stage, the so-called latent stage) is focused on the erogenous zone – the mouth, the anus, the phallus, or the genitals – that provides the greatest pleasure at that stage. Developmental progression may be disturbed at any time either by inhibition, that is, the failure to progress to the next developmental stage, or by regression, that is, the lapse to an earlier developmental stage. The person then acts out behaviours and ego defences associated with the developmental stage in which he is stuck or 'fixated'. If, for example, he is fixated at the oral stage, then he might become verbally abusive and exploitative (oral aggressive), or suck him thumb, bite his nails, or eat, drink, or smoke excessively (oral dependent). This might explain why smokers who are trying to quit often end up overeating and putting on weight, or chewing gum and losing tooth fillings. Psychosexual regression is also thought to lie behind the so-called mid-life crisis: a middle-aged person is gripped with anxiety at the prospect of ageing and losing his libido and sexual appeal and opportunities, so he regresses to the early genital (or adolescent phase), neglecting some or all of his responsibilities, buying a fast car, getting a piercing or a tattoo, frequenting bars and night clubs, having one or several affairs with people half his age, and such like.

A good example of psychosexual regression from literature is our friend Holden Caulfield, the protagonist of JD Salinger's *Catcher in the Rye*, who is so afraid of becoming an adult that he reverts to childish behaviours so as to cling on for as long as possible to his childhood. Thus, in Chapter 9,

> *Sex is something I really don't understand too hot. You never know where the hell you are. I keep making up these sex rules for myself, and then I*

break them right away. Last year I made a rule
that I was going to quit horsing around with girls
that, deep down, gave me a pain in the ass. I broke
it, though, the same week I made it – the same
night, as a matter of fact.

Regression is not invariably a bad thing, and may be consciously exploited to rediscover different, freer and more primitive, modes of being and relating. Indeed, regression is commonly employed by adults to relate and empathize with children and animals, or for the purposes of enjoyment, play, or creativity. In *The Practice of Psychotherapy*, Jung himself argued that the regressive tendency need not be 'just a relapse into infantilism, but a genuine attempt to get at something necessary … the universal feeling of childhood innocence, the sense of security, of protection, of reciprocated love, of trust, of faith – a thing that has many names.' If regression, or indeed any other process that is used for ego defence, is *consciously* employed – whether for ego defence or any other purpose such as empathy, enjoyment, play, humour, inspiration, creativity, and even survival – then it stops being our unthinking master and turns into our good and faithful servant.

PART IIIB: EVASION THROUGH PEOPLE OR THE WORLD

In evasion through people, a person copes with uncomfortable feelings not by conceiving of things as other than they really are (evasion through fraud), nor by finding escape in his thoughts (evasion through fantasy), but by altering the nature of his interactions with others.

24. Socialization

A person might alter his interactions with other people by becoming more convivial, partaking in social gatherings, cultural events, religious celebrations, and so on, and more generally surrounding himself with acquaintances, friends, and lovers so as not to be left alone with his deepest thoughts and feelings. Over time, he becomes adept at attracting people into his orbit and might even acquire the reputation of a natural born charmer, socialite, or Don Juan, all of which also serves to boost his self-esteem.

Socialization should be distinguished from group formation, in which the person with fears of intimacy or sex surrounds himself with a coterie, often of people of the same sex. His 'gang' makes sex and intimacy conveniently difficult and, at the same time, provides a cover-up and consolation for their absence.

Similarly, a person who has been disappointed or traumatized by a sexual relationship with one sex may develop a close but non-sexual relationship with a person of the other sex (usually the same sex as him). This ego defence, called 'ipsisexual object choice', accounts for the husband who spends more time with his drinking buddy than with his wife, or the wife whose thoughts and cares are more with 'her best friend in the world' than with her husband. Alternatively or over time, the person might even change his sexual preference.

Ego defences often serve several (unconscious) purposes, not all of which need to be defensive. For example, as well as being a source of comfort and security to the husband, the drinking buddy may also be a means for the husband to spite and to manipulate his wife. Indeed, the drinking buddy might even be serving the wife's purposes by occupying her husband and keeping him and his cares far away from her person.

25. Garrulousness

A person may also alter the way in which he relates to other people. For example, the person may become more talkative (or garrulous) so as to fill in any thinking time; prevent or avert uncomfortable questions and threatening conversations; attract attention, approval, or sympathy; reinforce a certain false self-image; control or dominate other people; or an amalgam of some or all of these.

In addition or alternatively, he may talk about an issue or issues that are unrelated or only remotely related to the issue that is really troubling him, an ego defence called glibness. This often comes across as, well, glib – that is, irrelevant, insincere, or just plain boring – to the good listener, who may be trying hard to hear whatever it is that is not being said. But one has to tread carefully; if the person becomes (subconsciously) aware that he has been found out, he is likely to bottle up and perhaps even to start avoiding the company of the good listener.

Indeed, an alternative to becoming more talkative is to become more reserved and uncommunicative and even to retreat from social interaction. This ego defence, called reticence, represents an attempt to avoid being found out, together with the discomfort and embarrassment that being found out may imply. Reticence should not be confused with shyness, social phobia, or selective mutism, a disorder in which a person (usually a child) is unable to speak in certain defined situations but is able to do so normally in others. That having been said, all three of these conditions – shyness, social phobia, and selective mutism – can also be thought of in terms of ego defence.

26. Dramatization

There are a number of more specific ego defences that can alter the way in which a person relates to others, including, for example, 'passive to active', dramatization, and grandiosity.

If the person fears an act of aggression or rejection, he might deal with this fear by provoking or pre-empting it and thereby acquiring some degree of control over it. Examples of such so-called passive to active behaviour are the child who creates havoc because he is going to get punished or abused regardless of his good or bad behaviour, the teenager who 'dumps' her boyfriend before he does her, and the employee who resigns just before he can be given the sack.

Dramatization is thought to be especially prominent in histrionic personality disorder. People suffering with histrionic personality disorder essentially lack a sense of self-worth, for which they depend on the attention and approval of others. They often seem to be dramatizing or 'playing a part' ('histrionic' derives from the Latin *histrionicus*, 'pertaining to the actor') in a bid to attract attention, create an impression, and solicit approval, admiration, and even adulation. They may take great care of their physical appearance and behave in a manner that is overly charming or inappropriately seductive. As they crave excitement and act on impulse or suggestion, they can put themselves at serious risk of accident or exploitation, particularly of sexual exploitation. Unfortunately, their dealings with other people are soon unmasked as insincere or superficial, and this can naturally have serious repercussions on their social and romantic relationships. As they are sensitive to criticism and rejection and react badly to loss or failure, this 'wearing off of the spell' greatly distresses them. A vicious circle may ensue in which the more rejected they feel the more histrionic they behave, and the more histrionic they behave the more rejected they feel.

27. Grandiosity

Histrionic personality disorder often overlaps with narcissistic personality disorder, which is characterized by grandiosity rather than dramatization. The true narcissist harbours a strong sense of born entitlement, self-aggrandizing fantasies, and a craving for admiration. In severe case, he may be envious, lacking in empathy, and ready to exploit others in the pursuit of his impressive goals. Although he can be charismatic and charming, he can all too often seem self-absorbed, controlling, selfish, and insensitive. If he feels slighted or ridiculed, he might be provoked into a fit of destructive rage and revenge seeking. Such a paroxysmal reaction is sometimes called 'narcissistic rage', and can have disastrous consequences for those at whom it is directed.

In *The Picture of Dorian Gray*, both the characters of Lord Henry Wooton and Dorian Gray are strongly narcissistic. Lord Henry's narcissism is insightful and often quite charming, and no doubt similar to that of his creator and alter ego, Oscar Wilde. For example, in Chapter 1, Lord Henry says, 'I make a great difference between people. I choose my friends for their good looks, my acquaintances for their good characters, and my enemies for their good intellects. A man cannot be too careful in the choice of his enemies. I have not got one who is a fool. They are all men of some intellectual power, and consequently they all appreciate me.' On the other hand, Dorian Gray's narcissism is cold and destructive, leading, among others, to the suicide of actress Sibyl Vane. In Chapter 7, Sibyl tells Dorian that he brought her to 'something [higher] of which all art is but a reflection' and made her understand the nature of true love. Instead of feeling touched or flattered, Dorian angrily replies that Sibyl's poor acting on that particular evening has killed off any love that he might in turn have had for her. Such are his cold-blooded terms:

> 'Yes,' he cried, 'you have killed my love. You used to stir my imagination. Now you don't even stir my curiosity. You simply produce no effect. I loved you because you were marvellous, because you had genius and intellect, because you realized the dreams of great poets and gave shape and substance to the shadows of art. You have thrown it all away. You are shallow and stupid. My God! How mad I was to love you! What a fool I have been! You are nothing to me now. I will never see you again. I will never think of you. I will never mention your name. You don't know what you

were to me, once. Why, once... Oh, I can't bear to
think of it! I wish I had never laid eyes upon you!
You have spoiled the romance of my life...'

In a study dating from 2005, Board and Fritzon at the
University of Surrey found that histrionic personality
disorder and narcissistic personality disorder (as well as a
third personality disorder, anakastic or obsessive-compulsive
personality disorder) are *more* common in high-level executives
than in mentally disordered criminal offenders at the high
security Broadmoor Hospital. This suggests that people
commonly benefit from strongly ingrained and potentially
maladaptive personality traits. For example, people with
histrionic personality disorder may be adept at charming and
manipulating others, and therefore at building and exercising
business relationships. People with narcissistic personality
disorder may be highly ambitious, confident, and self-focused,
and able to exploit people and situations to maximum
advantage. In their study Board and Fritzon described
the executives with a personality disorder as 'successful
psychopaths' and the criminal offenders as 'unsuccessful
psychopaths', and it may be that highly successful people
and disturbed psychopaths have more in common than first
meets the eye. As the psychologist and philosopher William
James put it more than a hundred years ago, 'When a superior
intellect and a psychopathic temperament coalesce ... in the
same individual, we have the best possible condition for

the kind of effective genius that gets into the biographical dictionaries.'

More recently, in 2010, Mullins-Sweatt and her colleagues carried out a study to uncover exactly in what respect or respects successful psychopaths are different from unsuccessful ones. They asked a number of members of Division 41 (psychology and law) of the American Psychological Association, professors of clinical psychology, and criminal attorneys to first identify and then to rate and describe one of their acquaintances (if any) who was successful and who also conformed to Robert Hare's definition of a psychopath,

> ...*social predators who charm, manipulate and ruthlessly plow their way through life ... Completely lacking in conscience and feeling for others, they selfishly take what they want and do as they please, violating social norms and expectations without the slightest sense of guilt or regret.*

From the responses that they collated, Mullins-Sweatt and her colleagues found that the successful psychopath matched the unsuccessful one in all respects but one, namely, conscientiousness. Thus, it appears that the key difference between unsuccessful and successful psychopaths is that the one behaves impulsively and irresponsibly, whereas the other is able to inhibit or restrain (or perhaps even sublime, Chapter 30) those destructive tendencies and build for the future.

Narcissistic personality disorder derives its name from the Greek myth of Narcissus, of which there are several versions. In Ovid's version, which is the most commonly related, the nymph Echo falls in love with Narcissus, a youth of extraordinary beauty. As a child, Narcissus had been prophesized by Teiresias, the blind prophet of Thebes, to 'live to a ripe old age, as long as he never knows himself'. One day, when Narcissus was out hunting for stags, the mountain nymph Echo followed him through the woods. She longed to speak to him but did not dare to utter the first word. Overhearing her footsteps, Narcissus cried out, 'Who's there?' to which she replied, 'Who's there?' When she finally showed herself, she rushed to embrace Narcissus, but he scorned her and pushed her away. Echo spent the rest of her life grieving for Narcissus, until there was nothing left of her save for her voice. Then, one day, Narcissus became thirsty and went to a lake. Seeing his reflection in the water, he fell in love with it, not realizing that he had fallen in love with his own reflection. However, each time he bent down to kiss it, it seemed to disappear. Narcissus grew increasingly thirsty, but would not leave or touch the water for fear of losing sight of his reflection. Eventually he died of love and thirst, and on that very spot there appeared a narcissus flower (Figure 9).

Figure 9: *Narcissus pseudonarcissus* or daffodil. 'He whom love touches not walks in darkness.' – Plato, *Symposium*.

The myth of Narcissus has long evaded interpretation, and what could Ovid possibly have meant by it? Like many blind figures in classical mythology, Teiresias could 'see' into himself and thus find self-knowledge. This self-knowledge enabled him not only to understand himself, but also to understand other people, and so to 'see' into their futures. If asked to predict someone's future, he sometimes, reluctantly, uttered a vague prophecy. But what did he mean when he prophesized that Narcissus would 'live to a ripe old age, as long as he never knows himself'? Perhaps he just meant that Narcissus would live for a long time so long as he did not fall in love with himself. Or, more subtly, that once Narcissus 'saw' himself, that is, understood himself and others (including Echo's love for him), he would be such a different person as to no longer count as his former self, and so resurrect as a flower (a plant that has flourished). Echo too must have been looking for herself, which is why she was never anything more than an echo. For both Echo and Narcissus, love of the world (of beauty, of the other, and, in particular, of the beautiful other) represented the means to self-knowledge, self-completion, and self-fulfilment – which is why Echo withered away after having had her love spurned by Narcissus. By falling in love with his reflection, Narcissus not only received the punishment that he deserved for his lack of piety in the treatment of Echo, but also unwittingly exposed the love of the world as being nothing but, or the same as, self-love.

In his novel *The Alchemist*, Paolo Coehlo invents a continuation to the myth of Narcissus: after Narcissus died, the Goddesses of the Forest appeared and found the lake of fresh water transformed into a lake of salty tears.

> *'Why do you weep?' the Goddesses asked.*
> *'I weep for Narcissus,' the lake replied.*
> *'Ah, it is no surprise that you weep for Narcissus,'*

they said, 'for though we always pursued him in the forest, you alone could contemplate his beauty close at hand.'

'But... was Narcissus beautiful?' the lake asked.

'Who better than you to know that?' the Goddesses said in wonder, 'After all, it was by your banks that he knelt each day to contemplate himself!'

The lake was silent for some time. Finally it said: 'I weep for Narcissus, but I never noticed that Narcissus was beautiful. I weep because, each time he knelt beside my banks, I could see in the depths of his eyes, my own beauty reflected.'

28. Humour

Many of the ego defences that involve evasion through one's relation with the world, such as humour, asceticism, altruism, sublimation, and anticipation, are considered to be 'mature'. This is not only because they imply some of degree of insight, but also because they can be adaptive or useful.

Humour, for example, presupposes that the person is able to see the absurd or ridiculous aspect of an anxiety-provoking emotion, event, or situation, to put it into its proper context, and to reveal it to others in the benign and gratifying form of a joke. One way in which medical students and junior doctors cope with being bullied by surgeons is to tell jokes about them, and one joke that I remember well is this one. Mr Smith dies and goes to Heaven. At the Pearly Gates, St Peter stops him. 'Everyone's equal here,' he says, 'so I'm afraid you're going to have to join the back of the queue.' After about 30 or 40 minutes, a man wearing surgical scrubs rushes past and straight into Heaven, crying 'Out of my way, out of my way!' Mr Smith calls out to St Peter, 'What was that?' I thought you said that everyone's equal here.' 'That,' replies St Peter, 'was God … but sometimes he thinks he's a surgeon.'

Freud himself noted that there is really 'no such thing as a joke': if human beings are the only animals to laugh, with some going so far as to turn laughter into a form of art and source of employment, then this is no doubt because they have by far the most developed unconscious in the animal kingdom. The things that people laugh about most are their errors and inadequacies; the difficult challenges that they face such as personal identity, social and sexual relationships, and death; and incongruity, absurdity, and meaninglessness. These are all deeply human concerns and challenges: just as no one has ever seen a laughing dog, so no one has ever heard about a laughing god.

All this is not to deny that humour cannot serve functions other than ego defence, for example, relaxation, pleasure, courting, bonding, problem solving, truth revealing – but merely to say that ego defence is one of the functions of humour and quite possibly its central and defining function. In other words, a joke that did not contain or reveal some defensive operation may well be amusing but could not be truly funny – an imitation and not the genuine article, a poor likeness of the ideal form. In fact, it seems that the funniest jokes are those that both reveal and parody our ego defences: every time you hear someone laugh, I mean, really laugh, ask yourself, what actually is he laughing about? And then join in with redoubled laughter.

29. Asceticism

Asceticism is the denial of the importance of that which most people fear and strive for, and thereby the denial of the very grounds for anxiety and disappointment. If fear is, ultimately, for oneself, then the denial of the self removes the very grounds for fear.

People in modern societies are more anxious than people in traditional or historical societies, no doubt because of the strong emphasis that modern societies place on the self as an independent and autonomous agent. In contrast, our ancestors, who had evolved to live in a group, conceived of themselves less as independent, autonomous agents and more as part of a group, subsuming their ego or identity into the collective identity of the group. For them, the long-term survival or flourishing of the group took precedence over their individual survival or flourishing. This means that they thought of their deaths less as the end of their lives and more as a part of the life of the group, which it, unlike their individual selves, kept on enduring. This enabled them to focus more on the present moment and on being, and less on the future and on becoming, which is the ultimate source of all anxiety[22].

It seems to me that there are three principal scales of time, the present moment, a human lifetime, and the eternal. The problem with modern man is not so much that he situates himself in the future of a human lifetime, since he fears death far too much to do that, but rather than he does not situate himself in any of these three scales of time. Instead, he is forever stuck somewhere in-between, this evening, tomorrow morning, next week, next Christmas, in five years' time. As a result, he has neither the joy of the present moment, nor the satisfied accomplishments of a human lifetime, nor the perspective and immortality of the eternal.

In the *Bhagavad* Gita, the Hindu 'Song of God', the god Krishna appears to the archer Arjuna in the midst of the battlefield of Kurukshetra and tells him not to abandon arms but to do his duty and fight on. Arjuna should not be afraid because, as Krishna says, 'There has never been a time when you and I have not existed, nor will there be a time when we will cease to exist … the wise are not deluded by these changes'. Similarly, the 20th century philosopher Ludwig Wittgenstein noted in his famous philosophical treatise of 1921, *Tractatus*

---

22 Anxiety is always for something that is in the future, such that it is impossible – other than circuitously – to feel anxious about something that has already happened.

Logico-Philosophicus, that, 'If we take eternity to mean not infinite temporal duration but timelessness, then eternal life belongs to those who live in the present.' By denying the importance of that which most people fear and strive for, the ascetic not only denies the very grounds for anxiety and disappointment, but also reconnects with, and immerses himself, into the timelessness and universality of the human experience.

The pre-Socratic philosopher Democritus of Abdera, the founder of atomism, is sometimes called 'the laughing philosopher' and compared and contrasted with his forebear Heraclitus of Ephesus, 'the weeping philosopher'. Democritus' father was tremendously wealthy, but Democritus fritted his inheritance on books and learned travel, reputedly travelling as far as India and Ethiopia. He eschewed wealth and position for a good life and a prominent place in the history of human thought; he once said that he would rather discover one true scientific principle than become king of Persia. Throughout his life, Democritus was always ready to laugh at the foolishness of people, so much so, in fact, that he gave rise to the expression 'Abderitan laughter', which refers to scoffing, incessant laughter. Despite this, the people held him in high esteem, not least because they thought that he could predict the future.

Heraclitus was an aristocrat with a claim to be king (basileus), but he abdicated in favour of his brother explaining that he much preferred talking to children than to politicians. The Persian King Darius once invited him to his resplendent court, but he refused to go, sending off the reply, 'All men upon earth hold aloof from truth and justice, while, by reason of wicked folly, they devote themselves to avarice and thirst for popularity. But I ... because I have a horror of splendour, could not come to Persia, being content with little, when that little is to my mind.' Heraclitus was a misanthrope with no interest in the vast majority of people, whom he found to be singularly lacking in understanding, and whom he compared to cattle. He once wished the citizens of his native Ephesus great wealth as a punishment for their worthless lives. He eventually removed himself to the loneliness of the mountains, where he lived out his days feeding on grasses and elaborating upon his theories about the oneness and perpetual motion of being.

Another beacon of the ascetic life is St Anthony of the Desert, the 'Father of All Monks', who has the rare distinction of having lent his name both to an Oxford college and to a skin disease (St Anthony's fire or erysipelas). According to the *Life of Anthony* by the 4th century and near contemporary bishop St Athanasius of Alexandria, Anthony, having lost both his parents, renounced his inherited wealth and devoted himself entirely to religious exercises, heeding the supererogatory counsel of Jesus, who, according to Matthew 19:21, said to the rich man, 'If thou wilt be perfect, go and sell that thou hast, and give to the poor, and thou shalt have treasure in heaven:

and come and follow me.' After some years on the ascetic path, Anthony took up residence in a tomb near his native village. There he resisted the temptations and torments of the devil, an episode that has often been depicted in art – including by modernists such as Cézanne and Dalí. Demons in the forms of wild beasts attacked him in the tomb, occasionally leaving him bruised and unconscious and in need of care (Figure 10).

Figure 10: *The Temptation of Saint Anthony* by Martin Schongauer (1450-1491). Copper engraving.

167

Having spent 15 years in the tomb, Anthony retreated further and into complete solitude, secluding himself in an abandoned fort in the desert of Egypt and subsisting on nothing more than the food that pilgrims catapulted over the walls. After some 20 years, his devotees persuaded him to leave the fort to instruct and organize them, whence his epithet 'Father of All Monks'. He emerged from the fort not ill and emaciated as people had been expecting but healthy and radiant. He passed five or six years with his devotees and then once again withdrew into the Egyptian desert, to a mountain whereupon can still be found the monastery that bears his name, *Der Mar Antonios*. This time, however, he did consent to receiving visitors and even undertook some travels. In particular, he twice visited Alexandria, once in 311 to support the Christian martyrs in the persecution, and a second time near the close of his life in around 350 to preach against the Arians[23]. One must believe that austerity makes for longevity: Anthony died at the grand old age of 105, which in the 4th century must in itself have counted as a minor miracle.

Anthony's life may seem heroic, but it is not nearly so heroic as that of St Simeon Stylites, who, in the 5th century, lived for 39 years perched on top of a pillar (Greek, *stylos*) near

---

23 The Arians believed that Jesus was not the same as God on the basis that God had created him in time, a belief grounded on John 14:28: 'Ye have heard how I said unto you, I go away, and come again unto you. If ye loved me, ye would rejoice, because I said, I go unto the Father: for my Father is greater than I.'

Aleppo in Syria. Simeon had initially sought isolation on a rocky eminence in the desert, but pilgrims invaded the area and pestered him for his counsel and holy prayers. As he could no longer find enough time for his devotions, he felt that he had no choice but to create a small platform atop a pillar, this time trying to escape from the *hoi polloi* vertically rather than horizontally. The first pillar was little more than nine feet high, but was superseded by others with the last being over 50 feet and crowned with a small balustered platform. There, exposed to the winds and rains and the beating hot Syrian sun, Simeon delivered addresses, wrote letters, and admitted of visitors who ascended to him by means of a ladder. Each year, he passed the entire period of Lent without eating or drinking, to which deprivations he added the mortification of standing continually upright. When he became ill, emperor Theodosius sent three bishops to beg him to come down to earth and see a physician, but he elected instead to trust in God and made a swift recovery. Simeon inspired several other so-called pillar-saints or stylites to take up his very particular brand of asceticism, not least one St Alypius who stood upright for 53 years before his feet could no longer support him, after which, still atop his column, he lay on his side for the remaining 14 years of his life. Indeed, the fame of Alypius may well have eclipsed that of Simeon had the latter not had that which management consultants call the 'first mover advantage'. Four basilicas were built around Simeon's column, and the base of the column and the ruins of the basilicas can still be seen in the vicinity of Aleppo.

In his *History of the Decline and Fall of the Roman Empire*, the 18th century historian Edward Gibbon says of Simeon,

> *In this last and lofty station, the Syrian Anachoret*[24] *resisted the heat of thirty summers, and the cold of as many winters. Habit and exercise instructed him to maintain his dangerous situation without fear or giddiness, and successively to assume the different postures of devotion. He sometimes prayed in an erect attitude, with his outstretched arms in the figure of a cross, but his most familiar practice was that of bending his meagre skeleton from the forehead to the feet; and a curious spectator, after numbering twelve hundred and forty-four repetitions, at length desisted from the endless account. The progress of an ulcer in his thigh might shorten, but it could not disturb, this celestial life; and the patient Hermit expired, without descending from his column.*

---

24 Variant spelling of 'anchorite', a person who lives in seclusion out of spiritual motives.

30. Sublimation

The ego defence of sublimation is an important one, and is considered by many to be the most successful of all the ego defences. If a person feels angry with his boss, he may go home and kick the dog, or he may instead go out and play a good game of tennis. The first instance (kicking the dog) is an example of displacement, the redirection of uncomfortable feelings towards someone or something less important, which is an immature ego defence; the second instance (playing a good game of tennis) is an example of sublimation, the channelling of uncomfortable feelings into socially condoned and often productive activities, which is a much more mature ego defence.

Another example of sublimation is the person with sadistic or homicidal urges who joins the army to provide an outlet for these urges, or, like Justice Laurence John Wargrave in Agatha Christie's novel, *And Then There Were None*, becomes a judge who liberally awards the death penalty in murder cases. Right at the end of the novel, in the postscript, a fishing trawler picks up a bottle with a letter just off the Devon coast. The letter contains the confession of the late Justice Wargrave in which he reveals a lifelong sadistic temperament juxtaposed with a fierce sense of justice. Though he longed to torture, terrify, and kill, he could not justify harming innocent people; so instead he became a 'hanging judge' and thrilled at the sight of convicted (and guilty) people trembling with fear.

The Italian renaissance polymath Leonardo da Vinci arguably sublimed his homosexuality into his art. Leonardo never showed any interest in women and even wrote that heterosexual intercourse disgusted him. Perhaps unsurprisingly, he never married, and chose instead to surround himself with beautiful young men, in particular Salai (a nickname meaning 'little devil') and Melzi, both of whom Leonardo included in his last will. In 1476, at the age of 24, Leonardo was twice charged with sodomy, even though the charges were common in the Florence of the *quattrocento* and soon dropped for a want of witnesses.

As in his life so in his art: Leonardo drew many more male than female nudes, and gave much more careful attention to the male than to the female genitals. Many of the figures in his paintings appear androgynous, especially the *John the Baptist* who, complete with the fine curls of Salai, looks nothing like the biblical cousin of Jesus and everything like Salai or, indeed, Mona Lisa. And if that were not enough, there is also a drawing entitled *The Incarnate Angel* from the school of Leonardo that appears to be a humorous take on the *John the Baptist*, depicting John (and therefore Salai) with an erect phallus (Figure 11).

Then, in the no less famous *Last Supper*, Leonardo painted a female figure, often interpreted as Mary Magdalene, in the

Figure 11: *The Incarnate Angel*, School of Leonardo. Charcoal on paper. As can be seen, someone at some point has attempted to rub out the erect phallus.

privileged position to the immediate right of Jesus. However, it is generally understood that it is in fact St John who occupied this position. In the Bible, John 13:23, it is written (presumably by John himself, or else someone close to John), 'Now there was leaning on Jesus' bosom one of his disciples, whom Jesus loved.' And again at 21:20, 'Then Peter, turning about, seeth the disciple whom Jesus loved following; which also leaned on his breast at supper, and said, Lord, which is he that betrayeth thee?' In his *Spritual Friendship*, St Aelred, Abbot of Rievaulx in the 12th century, contrasts St John with St Peter. To Peter, he says, Jesus gave the keys to his kingdom, but to John 'he revealed the secrets of his heart'. 'Peter ... was exposed to action, John was reserved for love.' Whatever the relationship between Jesus and St John, for Leonardo to have placed a female figure in the place of St John in a painting of the Last Supper designed for the dining hall of a monastery[25] might be thought of as rather more than just poor catechism.

Another example of the sublimation of homosexuality is that of the middle-aged protagonist of Thomas Mann's novella *Death in Venice*, Gustav von Aschenbach. Aschenbach, who is no less than the *alter ego* of Mann, is a famous writer who is suffering from writer's block. While staying at the *Grand Hôtel des Bains* on Venice's Lido Island, he is taken by the sight of a beautiful adolescent boy called Tadzio who is staying at the hotel together

25 The monastery of Santa Maria delle Grazie in Milan.

with his aristocratic family. Aschenbach becomes increasingly obsessed with Tadzio, even though he never talks to him and still less touches him. Instead, he sublimes his longing, which he eventually recognizes as sexual, into his writing. Thus, in Chapter 4,

> *... he, in full sight of his idol and under his canvas, worked on his little treatise – those one-and-a-half pages of exquisite prose, the honesty, nobility and emotional deepness of which caused it to be much admired within a short time. It is probably better that the world knows only the result, not the conditions under which it was achieved; because knowledge of the artist's sources of inspiration might bewilder them, drive them away and in that way nullify the effect of the excellent work.*

31. Altruism

The ego defence of altruism can be thought of as a form of sublimation in which a person copes with his anxiety by stepping outside himself and helping others. By focussing on the needs of others, people in altruistic vocations such as medicine or teaching may be able to permanently push their needs into the background and so never have to address or even to acknowledge them. Conversely, people who care for a disabled or elderly person may experience profound anxiety and distress when this role is suddenly removed from them.

Altruism as an ego defence should be distinguished from true altruism, the one being primarily a means to cover up uncomfortable feelings and the other being primarily a means to some external end such as alleviating hunger or poverty. However, many psychologists and philosophers have argued that there is, in fact, no such thing as true altruism. In *The Dawn*, the 19th century philosopher Friedrich Nietzsche maintains that that which is erroneously called 'pity' is not selfless but variously self-motivated. Nietzsche is in effect agreeing with Aristotle who in the *Rhetoric* defines pity as a feeling of pain caused by a painful or destructive evil that befalls one who does not deserve it, *and that might well befall us or one of our friends, and, moreover to befall us soon.* Aristotle surmises that pity cannot be felt by those with absolutely nothing to lose, nor by those who feel that they are beyond all misfortune. In an interesting and insightful aside, Aristotle adds that a person feels pity for those who are like him and for those with whom he is acquainted, but *not* for those who are very closely related to him and for whom he feels as he does for himself. Indeed, says Aristotle, the pitiful should not be confounded with the terrible: Amasis[26] wept at the sight of his friend begging, but not at that of his son being led to death.

Altruistic acts are self-interested, if not because they relieve anxiety, then perhaps because they lead to pleasant feelings of pride and satisfaction, the expectation of honour or reciprocation, or the greater likelihood of a place in heaven; and even if neither of the above, then at least because they relieve unpleasant feelings such as the guilt or shame of not having acted at all. This argument has been attacked on various grounds, but most gravely on the grounds of circularity: altruistic acts are performed for selfish reasons; therefore they must be performed for selfish reasons. The

---

26 It is not clear to whom Aristotle is referring.

bottom line, I think, is this. There can be no such thing as an 'altruistic' act that does not involve some element of self-interest, no such thing, for example, as an altruistic act that does not lead to some degree, no matter how small, of pride or satisfaction. Therefore, an act should not be written off as selfish or self-motivated simply because it includes some inevitable element of self-interest. The act can still be counted as altruistic if the 'selfish' element is accidental; or, if not accidental, then secondary; or, if neither accidental nor secondary, then undetermining.

Need this imply that Aristotle is incorrect in holding that pity cannot be felt by those with absolutely nothing to lose, or who feel that they are beyond all misfortune? Not necessarily: although an altruistic act is often driven by pity, this need not be the case, and altruism and pity should not be amalgamated and then confounded with each another. Thus, it is perfectly possible for someone lying on his deathbed and at the very brink of death, who is *compos mentis* and whose reputation is already greatly assured, to gift all or most of his fortune to some deserving cause, not out of pity, which he may or may not be beyond feeling, but simply because he thinks that, all things considered, it is the right thing to do. In fact, this goes to the very heart of ancient virtue, which can be defined as the perfection of our nature through the triumph of reason over passion. The truly altruistic act is the virtuous act and the virtuous act is, always, the rational act.

32. Anticipation

But how should a person think rationally if his mind is nothing but a jumble of ego defences? How, in the language of Socrates, should he know good and evil and the affairs of states if he does not have insight or self-knowledge? It has been argued that the most mature of all ego defences is anticipation, which involves finding self-knowledge and, like Teiresias, using this self-knowledge to predict or 'anticipate' our feelings and reactions, and, by extension, those of other people. I do not agree that anticipation is the most mature of all ego defences, not on the ground that there are even more mature ego defences, but on the ground that it is not an ego defence at all. An ego defence is by definition blind and unconscious, and anticipation is anything but. So if anticipation is not an ego defence, then what is it? I suggest that it is at worst a coping mechanism (like, perhaps, insightful humour, asceticism, or sublimation), and at best the first step to change.

In the Ancient World, the greatest of all oracles was the oracle at Delphi, and inscribed on the forecourt of the temple of Apollo at Delphi was a simple two-word command, Γνῶθι σεαυτόν, 'Know thyself'. In the *Protagoras*, Plato relates the origin of this inscription. In the time of Solon[27], he says, the seven sages of Greece[28] 'met together and dedicated in the temple of Apollo at Delphi, as the first-fruits of their wisdom, the far-famed inscriptions, which are in all men's mouths – 'Know thyself' and 'Nothing too much'.' At the end of the *Greater Alcibiades* (Chapter 17), Alcibiades promises that he will, with the help of Socrates, take greater pains about himself so as to get the better of the other Athenian politicians. Socrates, although no doubt pleased with Alcibiades, points out that his true rivals are not the other Athenian politicians but the Spartan and Persian kings, and that they can only ever be overcome by pains and skill, and by following the Delphic imperative to find self-knowledge.

For centuries the study of Plato and Aristotle formed the backbone of any higher education in Europe and beyond. As I hope to have demonstrated here and there in this book,

---

27 In 594 BC, Solon was appointed as archon in Athens, and gained such a reputation for wisdom that he was given *carte blanche* to reform the city. He broadened political participation by extending the right to be elected as archon to anyone who possessed agricultural wealth, and established a council of 400 citizens called the *boule* which was to be elected annually from a larger popular assembly called the *ecclesia*. Despite the two-year Anarchy that followed ('Anarchy', i.e. no archons elected), Solon had laid the foundations for Athenian democracy.

28 Solon, Thales of Miletus, Pittacus of Mytilene, Bias of Priene, Cleobulus of Lindus, Myson of Chen, and Chilon of Sparta.

one cannot possibly underestimate the individual benefit of this study, nor overestimate the social loss of having had it expunged from curricula. In *The Art of Failure*, I argued that the best education is not that which enables a person to make a living, nor even that which enables him to make a social contribution, but that which inspires and enables him on the path of freedom and individuation, and which, in the longer term, leads to the fullest living and the greatest social contribution.

33. Fear and anxiety

Anxiety is the dizziness of freedom.

– Kierkegaard, *The Concept of Anxiety*

The very purpose of an ego defence is to protect the mind, ego, or self from fear and anxiety, such that a person cannot hope to understand and overcome his ego defences unless he can also understand and overcome his fear and anxiety. According to its medical definition, which though not especially insightful still is dimly illuminating, anxiety is 'a state consisting of psychological and physical symptoms brought about by a sense of apprehension at a perceived threat'. Fear and anxiety can be a normal response to life experiences, a protective mechanism that has evolved not only to keep us from dangers such as the edge of a cliff, bite of a snake, or spear of an enemy, but also – by priming our body for action and increasing our performance and stamina – to help us confront or escape from these dangers should they befall us regardless. To put it more tersely, the purpose of fear and anxiety is, quite simply, to save us from dying.

At the same time, severe or inappropriate anxiety can be maladaptive, and can even prevent us from doing the sorts of things that most people take for granted such as caring after our personal needs or enjoying the companionship of friends and family. Such pathological anxiety is very common, and usually presents in one or more distinct patterns or disorders such as phobic anxiety disorder, panic disorder, or post-traumatic stress disorder (PTSD). At the same time, each one of these anxiety disorders can be interpreted and understood in existential or life and death terms. Let us begin with phobic anxiety disorder. Common specific phobias such as phobia of spiders (arachnophobia), enclosed spaces (claustrophobia), heights (acrophobia), darkness (achluophobia), storms (brontophobia), and blood (haematophobia) are all for the sorts of dangers that commonly threatened the lives of our ancestors. In this day and age, made-made hazards such as motor vehicles and electric cables are far more likely to strike us than natural dangers; nonetheless, most phobias are for natural dangers, probably because manmade hazards have not had enough time in which to imprint themselves onto our genome. Moving on, panic disorder is defined by recurrent panic attacks during which symptoms of anxiety are so severe as to make a person fear that he is suffocating, having a heart attack, losing control, or even 'going crazy'. As a result, the person develops a fear of the panic attacks themselves, which, paradoxically, sets off further panic attacks. A vicious circle takes hold, with the panic attacks becoming ever more frequent and ever more severe, and even occurring 'out of the blue'. Just as in specific phobias, the ulterior fear in panic disorder is of death and dying, as it is also in PTSD. PTSD is brought on by a highly traumatic event such as a car crash or a physical or sexual assault, and is commonly seen in military personnel and victims of rape. Common symptoms include anxiety, of course, but also numbing, detachment, flashbacks, nightmares, partial or complete loss of memory for the traumatic event, and avoidance of reminders of the traumatic event. The symptoms of PTSD vary significantly from one culture to another, so much so that PTSD is often thought of as a culture-bound syndrome. Many culture-bound syndromes are essentially culture-specific anxiety disorders, which, like PTSD and other anxiety disorders, can be understood in existential terms. This is certainly the case with koro and susto, which I discussed in Chapter 7. A third example is dhat, which is seen in men from South Asia, and which involves sudden anxiety about loss of semen in the urine, whitish discoloration of the urine, and sexual dysfunction combined with feelings of weakness and exhaustion. Dhat may be rooted in the Hindu belief that it takes forty drops of blood to create a drop of bone marrow, and forty drops of bone marrow to create a drop of semen, and thus that semen is a concentrated essence of life.

Ego defences protect the mind, ego, or self from fear and anxiety, the ultimate basis of which is – as I have just demonstrated – none other than death. In my experience, the simple appreciation of this fact is often enough to relieve fear and anxiety, and certainly presents a much healthier alternative to repeat courses of tranquillizing drugs. If ego defences are intimately related to fear and anxiety, then this is surely because their function is to protect the self and, in so doing, to prevent it from disintegrating and symbolically dying. In Chapter 15, I argued that the self is nothing but an abstract product of our minds, a convenient concept of schema that enables us to relate our present self with our past, future, and conditional selves, and thereby to create an illusion of coherence and continuity from a big jumble of disparate experiences. This great narrative is in constant need of writing and editing; anything that contradicts or undermines it also threatens the very foundation and integrity of the self, and so gives rise to intense fear and anxiety. This fear and anxiety activates ego defences that in turn protect the self against the assaults of reality. But at the same time, they also prevent us from living in the moment, adapting usefully to our environment, and developing a richer, more complex, and more fulfilling outlook on life. The illusion of the self may appear comfortable, but it comes at the high price of greater fear and anxiety and hence of lesser consciousness, freedom, and self-determination (Figure 12).

Just as a person might be able to relieve his fear and anxiety by gaining an appreciation of its relation to his death, so he might be able to overcome his ego defences by gaining an

Figure 12: Statue of Krishna revealing his Universal Form to Arjuna on the battlefield of Kurukshetra. Photograph by Steve Jurvetson. 'When one sees eternity in things that pass away and infinity in finite things, then one has pure knowledge.' – Krishna, *Bhagavad Gita*.

appreciation of their relation to his symbolic death. As the 20th century philosopher Martin Heidegger put it, 'If I take death into my life, acknowledge it, and face it squarely I will free myself from the anxiety of death and the pettiness of life – and only then will I be free to become myself'. This task is the greatest challenge of all, with a number of philosophers arguing that the very purpose of life is to prepare for death[29]. In contemplating death, a person may come to the realization not only that his death is inevitable but also that his life is meaningless, which in some cases may lead him to adopt the depressive position (Chapter 9). At the same time, he may cling on to the cherished belief that his life is, if not eternal, then at least important or special. The inner conflict that this gives rise to is sometimes referred to as existential anxiety, an emotion so disturbing that most people avoid it all costs by constructing an inauthentic but comforting existence made up not only of ego defences but also of such things as bourgeois values, moral codes, habits, customs, culture, and perhaps even religion, which Freud intimated is nothing more than a carefully crafted coping mechanism for existential anxiety.

According to Sartre, by refusing to face up to death (or 'non-being', in Sartrean terminology), a person is acting in bad faith, and so living out a life that is inauthentic and unfulfilling. Facing up to non-being can bring a sense of calm, freedom, even nobility, but also a different kind of anxiety marked by

---

29 Plato takes this idea even further in the *Phaedo*, which was known to the Ancients as *On the Soul*. In the *Phaedo*, Socrates tells the philosophers Simmias and Cebes that absolute justice, absolute beauty, or absolute good cannot be apprehended with the eyes or any other bodily organ, but only by pure thought, that is, with the mind or soul. For this reason, the philosopher seeks in as far as possible to separate his soul from his body and to become pure soul. As death is the complete separation of the soul from the body, the philosopher aims at death, and indeed can be said to be almost dead.

insecurity, loneliness, and responsibility. Rather than being a sign of debility, this existential anxiety is a sign of health, strength, and courage, and, above all, a harbinger of better and greater things to come. For the 20th century theologian Paul Tillich, refusing to face up to death not only leads to a life that is inauthentic, but also to neurotic (that is, pathological) anxiety. According to this outlook, pathological forms of anxiety such as phobic anxiety disorders and panic disorder arise from repressed existential anxiety, which itself arises from our uniquely human capacity for self-consciousness. By facing up to death and accepting its inevitability – a process that is facilitated by the adoption of the model of the self presented in Chapter 15 – a person is able to cure himself of fear and anxiety and, for the very first time, to put his life into perspective, see it in its entirety, and lend it a sense of direction and unity. In sum, it is only by integrating death into life that a person can free himself from fear and anxiety and, in so doing, to free himself to make the most out of his life and out of himself.

PART V: PROJECTION

The three majors groups of ego defences that have so far been examined are (1) abstraction, which involves ignoring or suppressing the source of anxiety so that it no longer seems to exist, (2) transformation, which involves converting the anxiety into some more manageable form, and (3) evasion which involves distracting oneself from the anxiety so as to minimize its threat and impact. The fourth and last major group of ego defences, projection, involves externalizing the anxiety and then dealing (or not dealing with it) in that form.

34. Projection

The ego defence of projection involves the attribution of one's unacceptable thoughts and feelings to others. For example, at an unconscious level a man may find himself attracted to another man, but at a conscious level he may find this attraction completely unacceptable. To diffuse the anxiety that arises from this conflict, he may transfer or 'project' his attraction onto somebody else and then berate *him* for being 'gay'. This is common playground behaviour in schoolboys, who can teach us much through retorts such as 'mirror, mirror' and 'what you say is what you are'. In addition to using projection, the man is likely to use a number of other ego defences, for example, repression (by 'forgetting' that he is attracted to a man) and reaction formation (by superficially overacting heterosexual). Notice that projection necessarily involves repression as a first step, since unacceptable thoughts and feelings must be repudiated before they can be attributed to others.

By projecting uncomfortable thoughts and emotions onto somebody else, a person is able not only to distance himself from those thoughts and feelings, but also, in many cases, to play them out vicariously and even to use them in the service of his ego. Thus, the man who projects his homosexual attraction onto somebody else is able not only to distance himself from his impulse, but also to keep it near the front of his mind (albeit in the disguised form of being somebody else's); moreover, by berating his target for being 'gay', he is reassuring himself and convincing others that he is not and could not possibly be homosexual, and so reinforcing his heterosexual self-construct. Other examples of projection include the envious person who thinks that everyone envies him; the covetous person who lives in constant fear of being robbed; the person with thoughts of infidelity who imagines that his partner is having an affair; and, on a much larger and more destructive scale, the insecure people who, in the 1930s and 1940s, conceived of the Jews as guilty and inferior and then persecuted them on that basis (see scapegoating, Chapter 10).

Projection is thought to be the principal ego defence in paranoid personality disorder, which is characterized by a pervasive distrust of others, including even of friends, family, and partner. As a result, the person is guarded and suspicious and constantly on the lookout for clues or suggestions to validate his fears. He also has a strong sense of his personal rights: he is overly sensitive to setbacks and rebuffs, easily feels shame and humiliation, and persistently bears grudges. Unsurprisingly, then, he tends to withdraw from others and to have great difficulty in building close or meaningful relationships.

Projection also underlies the phenomenon of transference, first identified by Freud in the context of psychoanalysis. Transference describes the tendency for a patient in psychotherapy to relate to the psychotherapist as he does or did to some other important person in his life, having projected this older relationship onto his relationship with the psychotherapist. If, for example, the psychotherapist is a man and the patient is a woman, then the patient is likely to (in at least some respects) re-enact her relationship to the significant men in her life, and so to men in general, with the psychotherapist. If, for example, she has an issue with trusting men that stems from the early unreliability or absence of her father, then she is likely to find it difficult to trust the psychotherapist. The psychotherapist should seize on this transference and explore it further, since it is likely to underlie the patient's likely history of short-lived and unfulfilling romantic relationships. Indeed, the recognition and exploration of the transference relationship often forms an important part of the process of psychodynamic psychotherapy. Other common patterns of transference in the clinical setting include love, parentification, dependence, anger, and hatred.

Of course, 'transference' can and does also happen outside the clinical setting, with people commonly projecting their feelings for a parent or ex-partner onto their current partners and children and, indeed – although to a much lesser extent – onto most anyone else. Thus, a young man who is angry with his father for having cheated on his mother might take this anger out on an older male friend (projection, displacement) and at the same time become very protective of his girlfriend and female friends (previous identification with the father, reaction formation). A similar process underlies the phenomenon of 'love at first sight', which usually involves the projection of an idealized love object onto a stranger with some superficial resemblance to that love object.

If transference can be defined as the projection by the patient of an older relationship onto his current relationship with the psychotherapist, then countertransference can be defined as the psychotherapist's reaction to the patient's transference. For example, if a female patient subconsciously treats the psychotherapist as she did her father, then the psychotherapist might start responding to her as her father did and/or as he (the psychotherapist) does to his daughter. If a patient is subconsciously seducing the psychotherapist, then the psychotherapist might well fall in love with the patient. It goes without saying that the psychotherapist needs to be just as attuned to the countertransference as he is to the transference, not only because this can help him to regulate his affects and impulses, but also because it can shed light on the transference and can be explored in therapy. For example, based on the countertransference, the psychotherapist might venture something like, 'I felt a little bit angry with you then. I wonder why that is.'

35. Projective identification

Then there is another, special form of projection. Projective identification is a primitive, non-verbal mode of relating to others that involves the projection of parts of the self onto another such that he feels pressured to think, feel, and act in accordance with the projection.

The recipient of projective identification ends up experiencing the psychic material *in lieu* of the person to whom it belongs and who is himself unable to access it. Unlike with simple projection, the recipient can temporarily lose insight and, like a puppet on strings, begin to experience strong feelings that are fundamentally alien to him. Through this process, the projective identification becomes self-fulfilling, and the source of the projective identification is able to distract himself with the frenzied reactions of the recipient.

An example of projective identification is a man with unconscious feelings of sexual inadequacy who makes his partner feel sexually inadequate. Another example is a psychiatric inpatient with unconscious feelings of helplessness who makes the doctors and nurses feel that they are incompetent and out of control. Of course, the doctors and nurses could develop insight into this particular instance of projective identification and attempt to resist it. In that case, they would most likely experience varying degrees of something like guilt, and the patient would most likely respond by intensifying the projective identification and perhaps even flying into a rage.

Note that projection and projective identification also serve a number of happier functions than defending the ego, such as assisting a baby in communicating with its mother and facilitating feelings such as pity, empathy, attraction, and love.

36. Idealization

The eponymous hero – or antihero – of Miguel de Cervantes's *Don Quixote* idealizes his 'princess' to such an extent that it becomes comical. To emulate the knights-errant of old who fought battles to earn the affections of their true love, Don Quixote identifies a simple peasant girl called Aldonza Lorenzo, changes her name to the much more romantic and aristocratic sounding 'Dulcinea del Toboso', and then paints her in the most flattering terms possible – even though he has only ever seen her fleetingly and never spoken to her. Dulcinea barely exists, but the idea of her nonetheless keeps Don Quixote alive on his quest.

> *...her name is Dulcinea, her country El Toboso, a village of La Mancha, her rank must be at least that of a princess, since she is my queen and lady, and her beauty superhuman, since all the impossible and fanciful attributes of beauty which the poets apply to their ladies are verified in her; for her hairs are gold, her forehead Elysian*

> *fields, her eyebrows rainbows, her eyes suns, her*
> *cheeks roses, her lips coral, her teeth pearls, her*
> *neck alabaster, her bosom marble, her hands ivory,*
> *her fairness snow, and what modesty conceals*
> *from sight such, I think and imagine, as rational*
> *reflection can only extol, not compare.*

Like the positive end of splitting (see Chapter 20), idealization involves overestimating the positive attributes of a person, object, or idea and underestimating the negative attributes; but more fundamentally, it involves the projection of our needs and desires onto that person, object, or idea. The classic example of idealization is that of being infatuated, when love is confused with the need to love, and the idealized person's negative attributes are not only underestimated but turned into positive attributes and thought of as endearing. Although this can make for a rude awakening, there are few better ways of relieving our existential anxiety than by manufacturing something that is 'perfect' for us, be it a piece of equipment, a place, country, person, or god.

But even a god is not enough. According to the 4th and 5th century philosopher and theologian St Augustine (Figure 13), man is prone to a curious feeling of dissatisfaction and to a subtle sense of longing for something undefined. This feeling of dissatisfaction arises from his fallen condition: although he has an innate potential to relate to God or the absolute, this potential can never be fully realized, and so he yearns for other things to fill its place. Yet these other things do not satisfy, and he is left with an insatiable feeling of longing – longing for something that cannot be spoken. The 20th century writer CS Lewis calls this feeling of longing 'joy', which he describes as 'an unsatisfied desire which is itself more desirable than any other satisfaction', and which I like to think of – in the broadest sense – as a sort of aesthetic and creative reservoir. The paradox of 'joy' arises from the self-defeating nature of human desire, which might be thought of as nothing more or less than a desire for desire, a longing for longing. In *The Weight of Glory*, Lewis illustrates this from the age-old quest for beauty,

> *The books or the music in which we thought the beauty was located will betray us if we trust to them; it was not in them, it only came through them, and what came through them was longing. These things – the beauty, the memory of our own past – are good images of what we really desire; but if they are mistaken for the thing itself they turn into dumb idols, breaking the hearts of their worshippers. For they are not the thing itself; they are only the scent of a flower we have not found, the echo of a tune we have not heard, news from a country we have not visited.*

Figure 13: *Saint Augustine in his Study* by Sandro Botticelli (1480). Fresco. *Desiderium sinus cordis*: Longing makes the heart grow deep.

Idealization is thought to be particularly prominent in dependent personality disorder, which is characterized by a lack of self-confidence and an excessive need to be taken care of. The person needs a lot of help to make everyday decisions and needs important life decisions to be taken for him. He greatly fears abandonment and may go through considerable lengths to secure and maintain relationships. A person with dependent personality disorder sees himself as inadequate and helpless, and so abdicates self-responsibility and turns his fate to one or more protective others; he imagines that he is at one with these protective others whom he idealizes as being competent and powerful, and towards whom he behaves in a manner that is ingratiating and self-effacing. People with dependent personality disorder often assort with people with a cluster B personality disorder[30] who feed from the unconditional high regard in which they are held. Overall, people with dependent personality disorder maintain a naïve and child-like attitude, and have limited insight into either themselves or others. This not only reinforces their lack of self-confidence and excessive need to be taken care of, but also leaves them vulnerable to abuse or exploitation.

A possible example of idealization in the context of dependence on a person with a cluster B personality disorder is that of Rosemarie Fritzl. For 24 years to 2008, Rosemarie's husband Josef Fritzl had been imprisoning and physically and sexually abusing their daughter Elisabeth in the basement of their

---

30 According to the American classification of mental disorders (DSM-IV), cluster B personality disorders comprise narcissistic personality disorder, histrionic personality disorder, borderline personality disorder, and antisocial personality disorder (including psychopathy, which is not a DSM label).

family home in Amstetten, Austria. Josef had fathered seven children by Elisabeth, of which one had died and three had remained in the cellar with Elisabeth. Despite Josef's secretive movements in and out of the cellar, his 1967 conviction for an unrelated rape, and the appearance of three children on her doorstep, Rosemarie, it seems, had never dreamt of suspecting him for the disappearance of their daughter.

37. Devaluation

The ego defence of devaluation can, at least in some respects, be thought of as the opposite of idealization. Devaluation is the attribution of unjustified or exaggerated negative qualities to someone or something. It can be employed to bolster one's self-esteem at the expense of others or as a form of projection to help conceal one's negative qualities. It can also be employed to minimize someone or something that represents a threat to our equilibrium, such as a psychotherapist who is 'useless', a successful friend who 'doesn't deserve his luck', or a relative with good but hard advice – or simply with the truth – who is 'unfair'. From then on, almost anything that the psychotherapist, friend, or relative can say or do is interpreted in the light of his being useless, undeserving, or unfair. Idealization and devaluation may go hand in hand, as in, for example, friends and enemies, heroes and villains. An interesting thought is that, whereas devaluation can remove us from the truth, idealization can tie us up to a falsehood and set us up for bitter disappointment and even, in some cases, half or an entire lifetime of constraint, boredom, and stagnation. This brings into mind an old quotation from the *Tale of Zummurud and Ali-Shar* in the *Arabian Nights*,

On the black road of life think not to find
Either a friend or lover to your mind;
If you must love, oh then, love solitude,
For solitude alone is true and kind.

38. Identification

Identification, also sometimes called or assimilated with incorporation or introjection (the subtle nuances in the nomenclature do not really matter to us), can be thought of as the opposite of projection, and involves the internalization of an aspect or attribute of another person.

Identification is not solely an ego defence, but also a normal and necessary part of human development. In fact, Freud originally distinguished three main kinds of identification. First, the original and primitive form of emotional attachment to parental figures by which the child experiences his parents as part of himself and thereby comes to share in their values and, by extension, in the values of his society. Second, a form of regression to this childhood state resulting from the loss, distancing, or unavailability of a loved one, for example, taking up the habits and mannerisms of a deceased parent or spouse. And third, a form of identifying and empathizing with others, particularly those with whom one already shares something in common. Since then, other forms of identification have been recognized. For example, identifying with an idealized person or fantasy; identifying with an aggressor and in turn becoming aggressive (as in the playground bully who has himself been bullied); and dedifferentiation, which refers to the process whereby one person becomes increasingly alike to another so as not to argue with or lose him, or perhaps just so as to relate better to him.

Identification can enable us to effortlessly appropriate a great deal from other people, simply by internalizing the better qualities of these 'role models'. But of course, life is seldom this simple. Today, whenever a person meets another with something that is highly valued such as position, good judgement, or tranquillity, the most common reaction is either envy or disdain (that is, devaluation, which in this case can be interpreted as a defence against envy). By reacting with envy, a person is unable to learn from those with something good or useful to teach him, and thereby condemns himself to a lifetime of stagnation. If he reacts instead with emulation, he is able to internalize the most admirable aspects of the more successful person and to move on to higher and better things.

According to Aristotle, envy is pain for the presence of good things in others, whereas emulation is pain for their absence in us. This is a subtle but critical difference. Unlike envy, which is self-defeating, emulation is a good thing because it makes us take steps towards securing good things. Emulation, says

Aristotle, is felt most of all by those who believe themselves to deserve certain good things that they do not yet have, and most keenly by those with a honourable or aristocratic disposition. The opposite of emulation is not envy but contempt, and those who emulate or who are emulated are naturally disposed to be contemptuous of those who have bad things or who have good things through luck rather than through just desert. There are three inferences that I can draw from all this. First, the way that we think about society has changed radically since the time of Aristotle, and not just for the better. Second, whereas emulation is the reaction of the few with high self-esteem, envy is the reaction of the many with low self-esteem. And thus that self-esteem is the key to self-improvement. As Aristotle said, pride is a crown of the virtues; it is not found without them, and it makes them greater.

Final words

Self-deception can have a number of benefits. Most obviously, of course, it can save a person from coming face to face with a painful truth. Although this truth might appear to be about another person or other people or about a certain situation or state of affairs, it is, in the final analysis, a truth about the person himself, and, moreover, a truth that undermines his sense of self. The undermining of a person's sense of self almost inevitably leads to uncomfortable or even painful feelings of fear and anxiety; this can sometimes lead to mental disorder, which in some cases can be thought of as a compensatory mechanism of sorts and in other cases (particularly depression) as a metaphorical disintegration of the self. Indeed, a person on the verge of mental disorder may be making frenzied use of his ego defences, with the resulting loss of perspective and/or function in itself counting as a mental disorder as, for instance, in some cases of dissociation, somatization, or reaction formation.

Although the primary purpose of self-deception is to save a

person from coming face to face with a painful truth, it can also serve a number of other beneficial purposes in the process. This is especially true of the most mature ego defences. Take, for example, asceticism. By denying the importance of that which most people fear or strive for, the ascetic is able not only to absolve himself from their lot of anxieties and disappointments, but also to search for a higher purpose and perspective, reconnect with the timelessness and universality of the human experience, and, paradoxically, receive the respect, admiration, and honours of the very people whom he repudiated. Or take sublimation. By channelling uncomfortable feelings into admirable pursuits, a person is able not only to expunge those uncomfortable feelings but also to make an easy and dignified livelihood and, in some cases such as those of Leonardo or Thomas Mann, even to find great fame and fortune. And take humour. As I have argued, the central function of humour is to reframe and minimize uncomfortable feelings, but in this process or by imitation of this process humour can also serve a number of other useful functions: creating perspective, of course, but also pleasure, relaxation, courting, bonding, problem solving, and truth revealing.

But it is not just the most mature ego defences that can serve a variety of beneficial purposes. Thus, a person who uses dramatization to attract attention and approval may be particularly adept at charming and manipulating others, and a person who uses grandiosity to fend off a depressive affect may at the same time discover untapped reservoirs of ambition and energy. So much is likely to explain the findings of Board and Fritzon that histrionic personality disorder and narcissistic personality disorder are both more common in high-level executives than in mentally disordered criminal offenders at the high security Broadmoor Hospital. It might of course be protested that it is not the personalities that are created around ego defences, but the ego defences that are created around the personalities. Thus, a person might have a predilection for using dramatization as an ego defence because he is already good at charming and manipulating others. Another person might instead choose grandiosity because he already far surpasses the average person in beauty, intelligence, talent, or some other domain. These things are obviously very difficult to disentangle. But let us grant that ego defences are indeed created around personalities and not *vice versa*. Even so, there are a number of ego defences that do not appear to be especially tied to personality and that can nonetheless serve a variety of beneficial purposes. For example, positive illusions are almost universally held. Looking at life through rose-tinted spectacles not only enables us to ignore painful truths, but also to take risks, see through ambitious projects, and cope with traumatic events. By lending a concrete shape to our feelings, the processes of symbolization and condensation also provide us with dreams and myths to enjoy, share, and learn from. Indeed, even in historical or traditional societies, man barely inhabits the physical realm, and moves instead in a hyper-reality made of the symbols that he has created. Idealization, on the other hand, may give us a goal to aim at and live for, and perhaps even our strong instinct for the absolute, infinite, and divine. So it is not just that ego defences may or may not provide us with one or several advantages, but also that they define our human nature and thereby frame the human experience.

Some authorities, in particular the evolutionary biologist Robert Trivers, have gone so far as to argue that natural selection favours self-deception, essentially because self-deception makes it easier to deceive others. By genuinely believing in an untruth, the argument goes, a person is more apt to convince others of that untruth because less likely to betray signs of deception such as clammy skin, excessive blinking, flaring nostrils, and so on. For example, a man with homosexual impulses might, through the ego defence of reaction formation, convince himself that he is heterosexual, in turn enabling him to better convince others of the same and avoid the costs of being perceived as a homosexual. To convince others of his heterosexuality, he may overact heterosexual by, for example, speaking in a gruff voice, mocking homosexuals and homosexuality, and engaging in a string of baseless heterosexual relationships, all of which would be rather more taxing and less convincing if were not a double deception.

Such, then, are the possible benefits of self-deception. But at what cost do they come? By removing us from painful truths, ego defences not only blind us to those truths, but also impair our ability to think rationally and therefore to reach the correct conclusions. Take, for instance, positive illusions. Yes, they may enable us to take risks and see through ambitious projects, but projects undertaken by people with a lack of perspective are nonetheless far more likely to fail than those undertaken by people with good insight and judgement. In this respect, ego defences are like a pair of crutches: useful to those with a handicap, but those without are much better off for not needing them. Take inauthenticity or bad faith. By sticking with the easy, unthinking, default 'choice', the person living in bad faith fails to entertain the multitude of other alternatives and possibilities that are open to him, and thereby reduces himself to the status of an automaton. If any more convincing is needed, just think of the truly tragic consequences that ego defences such as displacement or deanimation can have, not just for the person himself but for other people too, including even unborn people. For example, if a bank employee keeps on taking out his frustration on his 8-year-old son, the boy is left hurt and confused with his self-esteem damaged beyond repair. To cope with his poor self-esteem, the boy adopts a number of maladaptive patterns of thinking and behaving similar or different to those of his father. Many years later, he inflicts these upon his children, if only by his absence, and they too inherit and pass on and around their grandfather's original sin. In sum, no one could possibly doubt that conscious operations tend to favour more positive outcomes than blind, unconscious ones.

People who deceive themselves are, in the language of Socrates, people who do not know themselves, and people who do not know themselves can neither know their own good or evil, nor that of others, nor the 'affairs of states'. Anticipation is usually upheld as the most mature of 'ego defences' on the ground that it involves finding self-knowledge and, like the blind prophet Teiresias, using this self-knowledge to predict thoughts and feelings – a condition that is almost godlike not only in its wisdom, but also in the peace and tranquillity that it brings. Indeed, the ancient philosopher Epicurus of Samos argued that anxiety is the greatest obstruction to happiness; to attain a state of perfect mental tranquillity or *ataraxia*, a person needs to avoid anxiety, which he can do by learning to trust in the future. And what better way is there to trust in the future than to be able to read it? In contrast, a person who deceives himself is racked not only with fear and anxiety but also with an entire gamut of other psychological disturbances including anger, irritability, difficulty concentrating, insomnia, and nightmares. Not only that, but the thoughts, feelings, and behaviours associated with self-deception have a manic edge, that is, they are exaggerated, compulsive, and inflexible; the person is reduced to little more than some highly-strung marionette, with little of the capacities for consciousness, spontaneity, and intimacy that so define, elevate, and glorify the human experience. For these reasons, there cannot be any real tranquillity or happiness in self-deception.

As people who deceive themselves are left both with a defective and impoverished account of reality and with a restricted range of thoughts and emotions, they are far from fulfilling their full (cognitive and emotional) potential as human beings. This soon turns into a vicious circle, for the more constrained a person becomes, the less he is able to reason freely, and the less he is able to reason freely, the less he is able to overcome his constraints. Recall that for Aristotle, the distinctive function of human beings is to reason, and the Supreme Good, or Happiness, for human beings is to lead a life that promotes the development and exercise of reason. Reason begets freedom, and freedom begets reason, and both together beget knowledge of the truth, that is, wisdom, which for Aristotle is the highest happiness. The philosopher Diogenes the Cynic was a contemporary of Plato whom Plato described as 'a Socrates gone mad'. Once, upon being asked to name the most beautiful of all things, Diogenes replied *parrhesia*, which means free speech or full expression. The old dog used to stroll through Athens in broad daylight brandishing an ignited lamp. Whenever curious people stopped and asked what he was doing, he would reply, 'I am just looking for a human being.'

To summarize, a person prone to self-deception has a limited grasp on the truth and a restricted ability to reason, as a result of which he often makes suboptimal life choices; he also suffers from a range of psychological disturbances that remove him from tranquillity and happiness, and is impoverished and even dehumanized by a constricted range of thoughts and emotions. But there is still more. As much of his behaviour is defensively motivated, it does not 'add up' in the context of his bigger picture (in so far as he is capable of formulating a bigger picture), and appears to the insightful friend or observer as being unfounded, irrational, or idiosyncratic. In many cases, his behaviour is also dystonic, that is, out of keeping with his ideal self-image, and so all the more damaging to his deep-seated goals and ambitions and ultimately to the very sense of self that, through his self-deception, he is so desperate to uphold.

In the light of all this, I think that it is going to be difficult to argue that self-deception is or can be a good thing. This holds true even for the most mature ego defences such as asceticism, sublimation, and humour. If, say, St Anthony had just gone off into the desert without any insight into his reason or reasons for doing so, he may not have had the flexibility of mind to emerge from his fort to instruct and organize his devotees or to visit Alexandria to support the Christian martyrs. When understanding is lacking, goodness fails, and Anthony may well have passed over the opportunity to do the good deeds for which he is still remembered, indeed, venerated, as 'St Anthony the Great'. If a person with violent and homicidal urges ends up becoming a tennis champion but has only limited insight into his process of sublimation and generally into himself, then that makes his success less commendable because less deliberate. Moreover, his violent and homicidal urges remain not only unresolved but also untouched and unexplored, with a risk of returning with a vengeance once he is no longer a tennis champion. In Agatha Christie's novel *And Then There Were None*, the violent and homicidal urges of Justice Wargrave resurface after a lifetime of sublimation, leading to several grisly deaths including that of Wargrave himself. In Thomas Mann's *Death in Venice*, von Aschenbach, who is the alter-ego of Mann himself, ends up sacrificing a lifetime of discipline and dignity to pursue the young and beautiful Tadzio, extending his stay in Venice into an epidemic of cholera and dying from the illness. Finally, some uncharitable souls might say that, notwithstanding their unresolved homicidal or paedophilic urges, such one-dimensional, unreflective, and dysfunctional characters as our tennis champion, Justice Wargrave, and von Aschenbach could hardly make for inspiring company, not even to each other or, indeed, to themselves.

Self-deception is a defining part of our human nature. By recognizing its various forms in ourselves and reflecting upon them, we may be able to disarm them and even, in some cases, to employ and enjoy them. This self-knowledge opens up a whole new world before us, rich in beauty and subtlety, and frees us not only to take the best out of it, but also to give it back the best of ourselves, and, in so doing, to fulfil our potential as human beings. I don't really think it's a choice.

Epilogue

The world changes quickly,
like the shapes of clouds,
everything once finished falls
back to the ancient ground.

Far beyond change and progress,
greater and more free,
your early song carries on,
god with the lyre.

Pain has not been understood,
love has not been learned,
and that which leaves us in death

is not revealed.
Over the land all but the song
hallows and exalts.

    – RM Rilke, *Wandelt sich rasch auch die Welt*
    Trans. NB

Epilogue

Notes

Epigraphs

1.   José Ortega y Gasset, *The Dehumanization of Art and Other Writings on Art and Culture,* In Search of Goethe from Within, Trans. Willard Trask.

2.   Miguel de Unamuno, *Tragic Sense of Life*, The Practical Problem, Trans. JE Crawford Flitch.

Part I: Abstraction

3.   Fiona Barton, *Sisters keep mother's body in fridge for ten years – and visit every weekend,* Daily Mail, 6 September 2007.

4.   Elisabeth Kübler-Ross (1969), *On Death and Dying*.

5.   WR Miller and S Rollnick (2002), *Motivational Interviewing: Preparing People to Change*, 2nd Ed.

6.   Anna Freud (1936), *The Writings of Anna Freud.* Volume II: The Ego and the Mechanisms of Defense.

7.   Tom Leonard, *The 9/11 victims America wants to forget: The 200 jumpers who flung themselves from the Twin Towers who have been 'airbrushed from history'*, Daily Mail, 11 September 2011.

8.   Ilka Scobie, *Inside Man* (Interview with Eric Fischl), artnet.com.

9.   Plato, *Philebus.*

10. Plato, *Timaeus.*

11. Aristotle, *Nicomachean Ethics*, Bk. II.

12. Aristotle, *Rhetoric*, Bk. II.

13. Pliny the Edler, Natural History, 7:24.

14. Agatha Christie, *Sparkling Cyanide*, Ch 3. Spoken by Anthony.

15. Agatha Christie, *The Murder of Roger Ackroyd*, Ch. 12. Spoken by Hercule Poirot.

16. Leon Festinger, *When Prophecy Fails*.

17. Aesop, *Aesop's Fables, The Fox and the Grapes*, Trans. J Jacobs.

18. Aesop, *Aesop's Fables, The Lion, The Ass, and The Fox Hunting*, Trans. unknown.

19. Voltaire, *Candide: Or, Optimism*, Ch. 4, Trans. William F Fleming.

20. SJ Heine & T Hamamura (2007), *In Search of East Asian Self-Enhancement*, Personality and Social Psychology Review 11, 4–27.

21. Charles Darwin, *The Descent of Man*, Introduction.

22. J Kruger and D Dunning (1999), *Unskilled and Unaware of It: How Difficulties in Recognizing One's Own Incompetence Lead to Inflated Self-Assessments*, Journal of Personality and Social Psychology 77 (6): 1121–34.

23. David Burns, *The Feeling Good Handbook*, for the original (1989) presentation of the theory of cognitive distortions. Burns had then been working under Aaron Beck.

24. Oscar Wilde, *The Critic as Artist: With Some Remarks Upon the Importance of Doing Nothing* (essay in dialogue form).

25. Oscar Wilde, *The Critic as Artist: With Some Remarks Upon the Importance of Doing Nothing*.

26. The Bible (KJV), OT, Psalm 44.

27. Marcel Proust, *In Search of Lost Time / Remembrance of Things Past*, Vol. VI.

28. Marcel Proust, *In Search of Lost Time / Remembrance of Things Past*, Vol. II.

29. Marcel Proust, *In Search of Lost Time / Remembrance of Things Past*, Vol. II.

Part II: Transformation

30. John Aubrey, *Brief Lives, Sir Walter Raleigh*.

31. The Bible (KJV), OT, Book of Leviticus, Ch. 16.

32. The Bible (KJV), NT, Book of John, Ch. 1.

33. E Mostofsky et al. (2012), *Risk of acute myocardial infarction after the death of a significant person on one's life. The determinants of myocardial infarction onset study*. Circulation 2012.

34. Plato, *Charmides*, Trans. Benjamin Jowett.

35. Aristotle, *Nicomachean Ethics*, Bk. 8, Ch. 14, Trans. WD Ross.

36. Plato, *Lesser Hippias*, Trans. Benjamin Jowett.

37. Brian Ross and Maddy Sauer, *Foley To Resign Over Sexually Explicit Messages to Minors*, ABC News the Blotter, 29 September 2006.

38. Nils Bejerot: *The Six Day War in Stockholm*, New Scientist 1975, 61: 886, pp. 486–87.

39. William Shakespeare, *MacBeth*, Act V, Sc. 1.

40. Sigmund Freud, *New Introductory Lessons in Psychoanalysis*, Lecture XXIX Revision of the Theory of Dreams.

41. Carl Jung, *General Aspects of Dream Psychology*. In CW 8: *The Structure and Dynamics of the Psyche*.

42. Plato, *Politicus*.

43. Aristotle, *On Divination in Sleep*.

44. Philo of Alexandria, *On Sleep*, Bk. 1.

45. John Chrysostom, *The Homilies on the Gospel of St. John*.

46. Carl Jung, *Memories, Dreams, Reflections*.

47. The Bible (KJV), OT, Genesis, Ch. 1.

48. Voltaire, *Notebooks*.

49. The Bhagavad Gita, Ch. 2, Vs. 12.

50. Xenophanes quoted from John Burnet, *Early Greek Philosophy* (1930).

51. John Locke, *An Essay Concerning Human Understanding*. In the passage referred to, Locke defines a person as 'a thinking, intelligent being, that has reason

and reflection, and can consider itself as itself, the same thinking thing, in different times and places'.

52.   Sydney Shoemaker, *Self-Knowledge and Self-Identity.*

53.   Marcus Aurelius, *Meditations*, VII, 67.

54.   David Hume, *A Treatise of Human Nature.*

Part IIIA: Evasion through fraud and fantasy

55.   Sigmund Freud, *Civilization and its Discontents*, Ch. 3.

56.   Erich Fromm, *Fear of Freedom.*

57.   Irving Janis, *Groupthink.*

58.   Ilse Damme and Géry d'Ydewalle (2010), *Confabulation versus experimentally induced false memories in Korsakoff patients.* Journal of Neuropsychology 4(2):211–230.

59.   JD Salinger, *Catcher in the Rye*, Ch. 22.

60.   Miguel de Cervantes, *Don Quixote*, Pt. 1, Ch. 8.

61.   Miguel de Cervantes, *Don Quixote*, Pt. 1, Ch. 18.

62.   Shakespeare, *Anthony and Cleopatra*, Act II, Sc. 2.

63.   Lee Moran, *Thug who hit police officer with five stone concrete block thrown off building during Bristol riots over Tesco store is jailed*, Daily Mail, 18 December 2011.

64.   Angela Levin, *I was viciously raped on this Barbados beach but local police cared more about protecting tourism, says brave British grandmother*, Daily Mail, 30 November 2011.

65.   Philip Zimbardo, *The Lucifer Effect: Understanding how good people turn evil.*

66.   JD Salinger, *Catcher in the Rye*, Ch. 9.

67.   Carl Jung, *The Practice of Psychotherapy*, under *General Problems of Psychotherapy*.

Part IIIB: Evasion through people and the world

68.   Oscar Wilde, *The Picture of Dorian Gray*, Ch. 1.

69.   Oscar Wilde, *The Picture of Dorian Gray*, Ch.7.

70.   Belinda Board and Katarina Fritzon (2005), *Disordered Personalities at Work*, Psychology, Crime & Law, 11(1):17–32.

71.   William James, *The Varieties of Religious Experience*, Lecture 1: Religion and Neurology, Footnote 6.

72.   Stephanie Mullins-Sweat et al (2010), *The Search for the Successful Psychopath*, Journal of Research in Personality, 44:554–558.

73.   Robert Hare, *Without Conscience*, opening lines.

74.   Ovid, *Metamorphoses*, Book 3, Narcissus and Echo.

75.   Plato, *Symposium*.

76.   Paolo Coelho, *The Alchemist*, Prologue.

77.   The Bhagavad Gita, Sankhya Yoga.

78.   Ludwig Wittgenstein, *Tractatus Logico-philosophicus,* 6.4311.

79.   Diogenes Laertius, *Lives of Eminent Philosophers*, Trans. RD Hicks, 9.1, Heraclitus.

80.   St Athanasius, *Life of Anthony.*

81.   The Bible (KJV), NT, Matthew 19:21.

82.   The Bible (KJV), NT, John 14:28.

83. Edward Gibbon, *The Decline and Fall of the Roman Empire*, Ch. XXXVI, Simeon Stylites.

84. Agatha Christie, *And Then There Were None*.

85. The Bible (KJV), NT, John 13:23.

86. The Bible (KJV), NT, John 21:20.

87. St Aelred, *Spiritual Friendship*, 3.117, Trans. Lawrence Braceland.

88. Thomas Mann, *Death in Venice*, Ch. 4, Trans. Martin Doege.

89. Friedrich Nietzsche, *The Dawn* or *Daybreak*.

90. Aristotle, *Rhetoric*, Bk 2, Ch. 8.

91. Plato, *Protagoras*.

92. Kierkegaard, *The Concept of Anxiety*, p. 61.

93. The Bhagavad Gita, Ch. 18, Vs. 20.

Part IV: Projection

94. Miguel de Cervantes, *Don Quixote*, Pt. 1, Ch. 13.

95. St Augustine, *Confessions*.

96. Walt Whitman, *Song of the Universal*.

97. CS Lewis, *Surprised by Joy*.

98. CS Lewis, *The Weight of Glory*.

99. *One Thousand and One Nights*, Tale of Zummurud and Ali-Shar.

100. Aristotle, *Rhetoric*, Bk. 2, Ch. 11.

101. Aristotle, *Nicomachean Ethics*, Bk 4.

By the same author

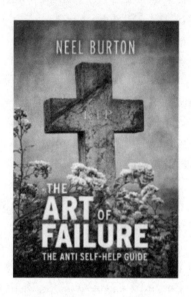

The Art of Failure, The Anti Self-Help Guide
ISBN 978-0-9560353-3-2

We spend most of our time and energy chasing success, such that we have little left over for thinking and feeling, being and relating. As a result, we fail in the deepest possible way. We fail as human beings.

The Art of Failure explores what it means to be successful, and how, if at all, true success can be achieved.

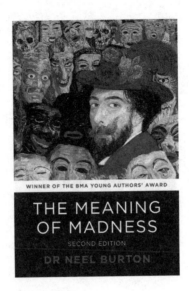

The Meaning of Madness
ISBN 978-0-9929127-3-4

This book proposes to open up the debate on mental disorders, to get people interested and talking, and to get them thinking. For example, what is schizophrenia? Why is it so common? Why does it affect human beings and not animals? What might this tell us about our mind and body, language and creativity, music and religion? What are the boundaries between mental disorder and 'normality'? Is there a relationship between mental disorder and genius? These are some of the difficult but important questions that this book confronts, with the overarching aim of exploring what mental disorders can teach us about human nature and the human condition.

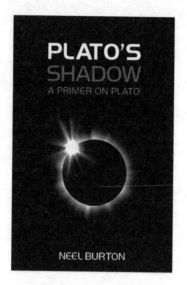

Plato's Shadow – A Primer on Plato
ISBN 978-0-9560353-2-5

Plato thought that only philosophy could bring true understanding, since it alone examines the presuppositions and assumptions that other subjects merely take for granted. He conceived of philosophy as a single discipline defined by a distinctive intellectual method, and capable of carrying human thought far beyond the realms of common sense or everyday experience. The unrivalled scope and incisiveness of his writings as well as their enduring aesthetic and emotional appeal have captured the hearts and minds of generation after generation of readers. Unlike the thinkers who came before him, Plato never spoke with his own voice. Instead, he presented readers with a variety of perspectives to engage with, leaving them free to reach their own, sometimes radically different, conclusions. 'No one,' he said, 'ever teaches well who wants to teach, or governs well who wants to govern.'

This book provides the student and general reader with a comprehensive overview of Plato's thought. It includes an introduction to the life and times of Plato and – for the first time – a précis of each of his dialogues, among which the Apology, Laches, Gorgias, Symposium, Phaedrus, Phaedo, Meno, Timaeus, Theaetetus, Republic, and 17 others.

Selected reviews

For the Art of Failure

An extraordinarily wide ranging mix of psychology and philosophy covering most of human behaviour from madness to happiness and the meaning of life, and encountering ghosts and death on the way. Neel Burton has already won several prizes ... and this volume deserves another.

The British Medical Association

This book saved my life.

Reviewer on amazon.com

For the Meaning of Madness

This book is a delight... there is no circumlocution or obliqueness, and the surgical efficiency with which the subjects are addressed makes for maximum comprehension... a really accessible and thorough approach to a complex and often impenetrable subject.

British Neuroscience Association

A life-changing eye-opener.

Reviewer on amazon.co.uk

For Plato's Shadow

A succinct précis of the work of one of the world's greatest thinkers ... For the newcomer or undergraduate it's a great resource, being both a celebration of and an introduction to some of the most remarkable, beautiful, provocative, powerful and vital writings in Western literature.

The Good Web Guide

If any one book is going to fulfil Alan Bloom's dream that all university graduates be acquainted with Plato, then this is certainly it.

Reviewer on amazon.co.uk

Index